POETRY NOW

BEHIND THE SPADE

Edited by Suzy Goodall

First published in Great Britain in 1994 by
POETRY NOW
1-2 Wainman Road, Woodston,
Peterborough, PE2 7BU

All Rights Reserved

Copyright Contributors 1994

FOREWORD

Although we are a nation of poetry writers we are accused of not reading poetry and not buying poetry books: after many years of listening to the incessant gripes of poetry publishers, I can only assume that the books they publish, in general, are books that most people do not want to read.

Poetry should not be obscure, introverted, and as cryptic as a crossword puzzle: it is the poet's duty to reach out and embrace the world.

The world owes the poet nothing and we should not be expected to dig and delve into a rambling discourse searching for some inner meaning.

The reason we write poetry (and almost all of us do) is because we want to communicate: an ideal; an idea; or a specific feeling. Poetry is as essential in communication, as a letter; a radio; a telephone, and the main criteria for selecting the poems in this anthology is very simple: they communicate.

Faced with hundreds of poems and a limited amount of space, the task of choosing the final poems was difficult and as editor one tries to be as detached as possible (quite often editors can become a barrier in the writer-reader exchange) acting as go between, making the connection, not censoring because of personal taste.

In this volume around two hundred poems are presented to the reader for their enjoyment.

The poetry is written on all levels; the simple and the complex both having their own appeal.

The success of this collection, and all previous *Poetry Now* anthologies, relies on the fact that there are as many individual readers as there are writers, and in the diversity of styles and forms there really is something to please, excite, and hopefully, inspire everyone who reads the book.

Contents

Villanelle: Darnell And All The Idle Weeds (In Praise Of The Hoe)	J R Holt	1
Flowers	Sally Lucas	1
My Garden	Eric Bennett	2
The Stone	Jeffrey Barham	3
The Tree	C A Lees	3
The Shed	Sonia Elliott	4
October	Chloe	5
Apprentice Gardener	F E Crisp	5
Ode To The Allotment Hut	Eric Knight	6
Four Golden Leave	Ian Clack	7
Fresh Hope	Dorothy Pothecary	7
The Rural Seasons	Sydney Webster Snr	8
Mid Life Crisis	May-Anne Watson	8
A Gardener's Nightmare	Sandra Farmer	9
Idyllic Gardening	Roger Stappleton	10
Summer Garden	Alison Newbould	10
Reflections	Patti Hinsull	11
Even Gardeners Get Fed Up Sometimes	James Nash	12
Happy Holiday	Desmond LePard	13
Limerick	M Humphreys	14
Untitled	David A Garside	15
Untouchable Sun	Mariza Arnold	15
Perennial Pest	Dora Roberts	16
Transformations	Valerie Hockaday	17
Adieu My Old Cottage Garden	Eric Smart	18
Autumn Beginnings	Homer	19
Autumn	Russel T Martin	19
The Seedling	Diane Sinclair	20
Brief Encounter	Alexandra McKenna	21
Gardening Groans	Brian Field	22
Carousel	Joan Evans	23
Sweet Cherry	Wilhimina Gilliam	24
The Gardener	Margaret Paterson	24
The Watering Can	Aileen North	25

Garden Solace	Brenda Larkin	26
Requiem For Spring Or The Flower Mugger	June Keal	27
Pilgrim Of The Year To Come	Roger Mansbridge	27
Jack's Delight	Sylvia Dunn	28
A Garden Verse	James McMillan	29
My Garden	Joyce Clifford	30
Poppadums and Marigolds	Barbara Johnson	30
Backyard Hotel	Val Pöhler	31
Disillusioned	Susan Chevalier	32
Gardening	Joan Ungemuth	33
The History Of The Rose	Jean Avery Wright	34
A Paradise	Doris Bowden	35
A Late Conversion	Jenny Ogilvie	35
A Gardener Grows Old	Robin Robbins	36
The Joys Of Gardening	Caroline Merrington	37
Garden In Winter	Ann Rawson	38
Gnomophobia	Valerie Edge	38
My Garden	Jean Hillier	39
Spanish Garden	Mary Ellis	40
The Rose Garden	Rosie A Rumble	41
Conservation	Emma Barry	41
Snowy Garden	Laura F Pocock	42
My Landrake Garden	Kay Tompson	42
Behind The Spade	Roy E Lewin	43
Behind The Spade	Irene Baker	44
The Ugly Bug Ball	Jean Roberts	44
Michael	Jane Spray	45
Untitled	Lynn Nash	45
The Garden - A Sonnet On It	Ian W Millar	46
To A Cabbage	Trevor Williams	46
Call Of The Wild	Peter H Adams	47
And Then Green Light	Martin Paul Smith	48
Explanation Please?	Minna Rickaby	49
The Flower's Lost Bloom	Rita Morgan	49
Miss Bonner Bakes Bread	Rebecca Farmer	50
The Wilderness	Brian L Giggins	51
Pest Aside	Cavan Syrad	51

Labour In Vain	R P Tonks	52
Worm Warning	Jack Rowe	52
Bees On Echinops	Joy Ginger	53
The Darkborn	Gordon Litchfield	54
Behind The Spade	Joan Bradshaw	54
Leaves	Alan M Kent	55
Paradise	Shelagh Stannard	56
Miracles	Paddy Jupp	57
All Fineness and Finery Goes To Earth	Clover	58
Bishopswood	S Bishop	58
Ode To The Anti-Gardener	Shirley Frost	59
A Blackbird's Song	J A Bush	60
Garden In The Dusk	Marion Robinson	61
A Tree	G Sandiford	61
Blue	Winifred Corrin	62
Nettle Rash	Roselie Mills	63
Self Heal	Doris Beer	63
A Garden	Jean Amor	64
To A Rose	Kathleen Cawley	65
The Kelsae Onion	Ian McPherson	65
The Secret Garden	Dorothy Bassett	66
The Garden In Autumn	Honey Wilde	66
Outside In My Garden	Mary O'Dyer	67
The Gardening Bank	A J Perry	68
Mollie's Climbing Rose	Louise C Evans	68
Gastropod	Richard Swale	69
My Sanctuary	Madeleine McWilliam	69
Dig For Victory	Deborah Hearn	70
Amanuensis Honorarius	Daphne Lawry	70
A Quiet Hour	Marion Henderson	71
Season's Beauty	H Bradford	72
God's Little Acre	Bobby Rashley	72
Conversation With A Blackbird	Lynn Gates	73
Dusk	Sue Chadd	74
My Garden	Jeanne Hollett	75
Little Hands	Mary Walsh	76
Nature's Return	Lorna May Noah	76

Title	Author	Page
The Garden Is ...	Kathryn A Booth	77
From Mother Nature	Katherine E Philp	78
The Gardeners' Resurrection	Ian Boddy	79
My Garden	Kathleen Leonard	80
Chocolate-Box Gardens	Rita Woodall	80
The Living Garden	Michael Staniforth	81
These Make Me Laugh	Dorothy Francis	82
Grandma Birch's Garden 1934	Eileen King	83
The Birch Tree	Phyllis Moore	83
The Struggle	Audrey Moody	84
My Birthday Present	S Neale-White	85
Garden Of Dreams	Keith Bowler	86
Autumn	Kate Brown	86
A Garden In Spring	A P Hilton	87
Treasured Memories	Rita Seward	88
Beauty Abounds	Jocelyn Banthorpe	89
Love Affair	Dorothy Dosson	90
The Formal Bed	James Walters	91
Short Lives	R F Trollope	92
The Garden Changes	Muriel Grindley	93
Love's Garden	Jill Collingham	93
In An Allotment Garden	Penny Lungley	94
In My Dream Garden	Rhona Anne Pointon	95
Behind The Spade	Valerie Jackson	96
Colour Coded	Hazel H Mingham	97
My Garden Shed	Monica Brooke	98
A Gardener's Dilemma	Vivienne Tuddenham	99
Untitled	Joan Letts	100
It's All Worthwhile	Angela Morley	101
Lawn Gems	Gwen Mason	102
Up The Garden Path	M Scofield Jones	103
Through The Garden Gates	G Coleman	104
The Green Look	Bill Johnson	104
Mi Yella Rose Bush	Esma Banham	105
Being Neighbourly	Olive Smith	106
Untitled	P T Dover	107
My Garden	Sheila Holligon	108
A Gardener's Dream	D M Lee	109

Rain	K Sutton	109
A Wildlife Garden	Pete Perry	110
How Many Times	Leslie William Bullock	111
My Neighbour's Cherry Tree	Mollie Bramble	111
A Seed	Horace Hartley	112
Dream Garden	Brian William Smith	113
The Garden Parade	Sarah Doyle	114
Gardeners' World	Betty Lightfoot	115
A Gardeners Lament	M A Read	116
October Garden	Dorothy Morris	116
The Fuchsia	Sarah Louise Appleyard	117
A Lovely Place To Be	Jean McDonald	118
Garden For All Seasons	Olwen France	119
Anticipation	Anne Aitchison	120
Untitled	P Sears	120
Untitled	Gugnunc	121
The Cheat	D Burns	121
Compromise	John Clifford	122
My Garden	Christine Morris	123
Strawberries	Barbara Ellis	123
The Passion For Gardening	S M Bell	124
Ferns	Jon Finney	125
Pests	Andrew Readman	126
More Than A Hobby	Louise Corbett	126
Behind The Spade	Barbara Voss	127
If It Wasn't For the 'Pillars In My Garden	V V Stauber	128
Growing Wild	Kim Hopkinson	129
Simply Nature	Alan J Cocks	130
Mealtime	Patricia Gray	131
Spring Time	T B Rees	132
The Allotments	Sue White	132
No Larger Than A Postage Stamp	Patricia Catling	133
Garden Gifts	Deidre Ann Bates	134
The Herb Garden	Ruth M Hart	135
Now Behind The Spade	Eddie Shaw	136
Behind The Spade	Cyril Harding	137

Garden Thuggery	M Hutchings	138
Leaning On A Spade	Patrick Taylor	138
The Conservationist	M Boreham	139
The Last Rose Of Summer	John Cotterill	140
Untitled	Alice Coles	140
A Garden Knows	Lynne Tice	141
The Gardener	Cynthia Byrnes	141
A Death In The Garden	Jenny Owen	142
A Special Thank You	Thelma Watson	143
The Spirit Of The Garden	W A Prescott	144
Colour In The Winter Garden	Christopher Lewis	145
The Gardener	Alison Hodge	146
The Gardener	Pauline Brennan	147
The Onion Grower	Dylan Pugh	147
In Our Garden	George Burns	148
A Gardener's World	G M Craske	149
The Garden	Eva Donaghy	150
New Garden	L J Culbert	150
The Allotment	Karen Hullah	151
Watching Bombus In July	Audrey A Greenleaf	151
The Failed Gardener's Lament	Mary Cameron	152
The Persimmon Tree	Phyllis Paynter	153
My Garden	W R Fyfe	154
Time Well Spent	Tessa Mondesir	155
Behind The Spade	Jennifer Jenkins	156
Garden Fantasy	Beryl M Smith	156
The Magic Garden	Mary Marriott	157
Our Garden	Diana	158
Within The Edges Of Mortality	Raymond Fenech	159
Gardening After Work	Peter Haslehurst	159
Garden Seasons	Mary Johnson-Riley	160
Our Garden	Edward Lea	161
Spring	F M Ayling	161
My Garden	Malcolm Richards	162
Seasons	M O Brazier	162
A Gardener's Lament	Christine A Goodhugh	163
My Mantra - The Garden	Deirdre van Outersterp	164
My Garden Plan	Mollie E Carter	164

Your Garden	John R Monk	165
My Pride And Joy	Hilda Greenhalf	166
Tunnel Vision	Ann Popple	167
Pruning	Cyril Mountjoy	167
Like A Poppy In The Field	Stina de Graaf	168
What A Challenge	Gwen Daniels	168
Though I Try	Derek Beavis	169
Nearer God's Heart	Yvonne Bulteel	170
Trees	Andrew Banfield	171
The Reluctant Gardener	Jenny Holmes	172
Taken For Granted	G Milne	173
My Garden Of Memories	Beryl Osborne	173
A Gardner's Acrostic	Aoife Toomey	174
Then God A Garden Made	Marion Brisley	175
Earth	Susanne Shalders	176
Behind The Spade	Cynthia Bach	177
The Perfect Garden	Helen Dodd	178
Childhood Memories	Terry Kearey	179
My Haven Of Peace	Sylvia Dodds	180
A Promise Of Spring	Michelle Loetz	181
The Garden's Our Pleasure	Muriel Cooper	181
Good Programming	Peter Cornaish	182
Destruction	Susan Mary Heggie	182
A Fleeting Visit	P J Reed	183
Untitled	Rachael Robinson	183
A Lily Flower	Jeanne Webb	184
The Soil	Liam Keating	185
Ode To A Tomato	Kate Roberts & Linda Terry	186
The Hidden Garden	Susi Howell	187
Of Moles And Men	C Gent Drummond	188

VILLANELLE: DARNEL AND ALL THE IDLE WEEDS
(IN PRAISE OF THE HOE)

Darnel and all the idle weeds that grow
in gardens and escape the poisonous spray
shall not evade my well-directed hoe.

It's January now when rain and snow
not only check the gardener but delay
Darnel and all the idle weeds that grow.

But spring is not far off and well I know
how many weeds will flourish then; but they
shall not evade my well-directed hoe

whether they be obnoxious or no.
A spring offensive must be aimed to slay
Darnel and all the idle weeds that grow

in any bed or border and, although
some may be obstinate, they must not stay -
shall not evade my well-directed hoe.

However gracefully wild-flowers may blow
and grasses flutter in the winds of May,
Darnel and all the idle weeds that grow
shall not evade my well-directed hoe.

J R Holt

Flowers
Just to lie in a suspended dusk
Perpetuate the softening sounds of birds
And slowly penetrate the outer husk
Of downy whole green summers cracked in words
And watch the waiting for the dew-wet gems
On creaking leaves and line of beckoning stems

As if the secret's in a dimming flower
Subtly with twilight lips indented;
In one mellow, elongating hour,
Jasmine, rose and honeysuckle scented,
Breezes pale as stocks on midnight air,
Can we remain awake or senses doze
And in an evening's enigmatic stare
Reflect an answer, as the sea
Mirrors the moon its endless tides obey,
Or are we trapped forever in a rose?

Sally Lucas

MY GARDEN

My garden is the envy of my neighbours, family, friends
It's my castle and my refuge, a means to all my ends

With everything you could desire, you name it, it is there
Not just for me but anyone, my secret you may share

To find the very place for you, a special spot to be
Not matter where, it will be there, for you alone to see

How far you walk is up to you, no need for it to end
Your choice to sit and rest a while, no reason to defend

Those aching legs or tired feet, these happen to us all
The decision yours entirely which memories you recall

The secret that I now reveal is simple to explain
If I tell you that my garden is really very plain

It only covers ten square yards and has a boundary wall
It faces north with little sun and has no view at all

There also are no lawns to mow or weeds to be controlled
No rush to cover bedding plants should evening be too cold

It's there to meet my every wish when just to close my eyes
Is all I ever need to do to make it paradise.

Eric Bennett

THE STONE

While walking on the seashore
I found a strange-formed stone,
Washed by countless tidewaves
Worn through long ages gone.
I brought it home that evening,
This sea-shaped thing I'd found,
And in my garden placed it
And planted flowers around.
One winter's morn I found it,
And in two parts it lay.
For with the frost it shattered
When the sunlight broke the day.
This stone deformed by nature
Long nature's seal had borne -
A shining whirling fossil,
Unseen since old earth's dawn.

Jeffrey Barham

THE TREE

Its spreading canopy towers above my head,
Its heavy leaves hanging down like lead,
The new born flowers bursting from bud,
The nettles below springing from the mud.

Its glorious crown spreading out so wide,
Its rugged, fat torso where all can hide,
The roots digging deeper to anchor it down,
The bark with its knots all silver and brown.

A heart with two names on is etched in the skin,
Did she or didn't she really love him?
Who knows the answer perhaps just the tree,
Its golden heart so open and free.

Its spreading branches quiver by my feet,
It heavy leaves all crumpled not neat,
The life taken swiftly with petrol and saw,
Its dying torso lies on the floor.

The roots still dig deeply but don't anchor down,
The white innards split not silver or brown,
A heart with two names on, no longer is seen,
Just a pile of sawdust where man has been.

C A Lees

THE SHED

Half packets of seeds
Next years beans.
Killer for weeds
And fluid that cleans.

Old wooden trug
Gardening hints.
Broken stool
And honing flints.

Well oiled tools
Tobacco tins.
Broken stool
And knotted strings.

Assorted jars
Pocket knife.
Old crowbars
Memories are rife.

Half a century
In an old man's shed.
Children to be told
Their Grandad's dead.

Sonia Elliott

OCTOBER

Resplendent Sumach, gold and green and wine
A graceful feathered canopy
Holds high aristocratic candlesticks
Plush plumes of velour burgundy.

The swelling yellow Quince hangs tempting by
Its heady perfume overpowering all
Great goodly mushrooms spring from stippled shade
And emerald mossy cushions hug the wall.

Time now to wash the pots and sweep the stone
To tidy, layer, burn; to stack and store
An ever-deepening carpet softly builds
As swirls of amber leaves float to the floor.

Chloe

APPRENTICE GARDENER

Gardening isn't partic'ly unpleasant
If you discount the backache and stings
From the nettles and bees
And the pain in your knees
When you kneel down to pull out the weeds.

No, it's quite enjoyable really,
Providing the weather is fine,
If it's not snowing
And the wind isn't blowing
And the mud isn't up to your knees.
And I think it's really quite smashing
To germinate something from seed;
Radish or oregano?
Well, how should I know
The wind blew the instructions away!

Of course, I *am* only learning,
And I know that my knowledge is thin,
But I read all the books
And I get funny looks
At the nursery, out in the rain.

But I won't let this mystery beat me,
I shall grow all those *difficult* things:
Primrose and azalea,
Orchid and camellia -
and I'll display at the RHS!

F E Crisp

ODE TO THE ALLOTMENT HUT

Abandon hope, all who enter here,
No whisky, gin or even beer.
It's a bit of a dog house in which to hide,
From irate wife, on the nagging side.
Queue up here for spud advice
How to plant 'em, cor! That's nice.
How to till, prepare your ground,
Not planting shallots upside down.
Somewhere to sit if feeling ill,

Or for a cuddle with Dibber Lill.
And when you die, t'will be just great,
Where allotment holders lie in state.

Eric Knight

FOUR GOLDEN LEAVES

Four golden leaves
In perfect symmetry
Gracefully hang
Defying winters harsh reality
I noticed them one day, or did they notice me?
Four golden leaves in perfect symmetry.

Ian Clack

FRESH HOPE

The plant which gave such joy when seen on sale
Sometimes seems so unhappy in our garden.
Making us wonder if we have chosen rightly.
Yet, given time, tiny fresh leaves appear,
The stem grows strong and we feel the wonder
That time has reconciled the newcomer
To be at one with us to share its beauty.

Dorothy Pothecary

THE RURAL SEASONS

Rustic red soil and grasses so green,
Are all part of nature's seasonal scene,
Sentry like trees and mossy fur flora,
Are creature love nests and provender for fauna.
Rain soaked mountains and sun kissed land,
Creator of rivers and gold grains of sand.
Winter caresses the trees with white dresses,
Spring perfumes the air from blossom of sweet pear.
Summer morn dew clings to grasses that glisten
Birds on stout oak observe and listen,
Autumn leaves crinkle and flutter around,
Collecting in nooks forming small mounds.
Our countryside patterns of all shades of hue,
Enhances the richness of Britain so true.

Sydney Webster Snr

MID LIFE CRISIS

Our garden could be magical,
Our garden could be fun.
Instead, it's just a large green space
where children used to run!

An interesting path could wind around just over there
and then we'd have to place to sit. We'd contemplate and stare
at fish that glide around 'neath lily pads and flowers,
and watch the bees and hover flies at work around the bowers
where roses bloom, and honeysuckle, lavender and thyme
and lilies in profusion, giving off a scent sublime.

Our garden is a lovely space
of clear uncluttered green.
She wants to fill it up, you know.
it's ghastly! Well . . . I mean! . . .

A pond that will go slimy and in summer start to smell;
a trellis, and an orchard and a pergola as well!
Behind us there are playing fields and miles and miles of sky.
She wants to block it out with trees and climbers growing high!
Then the roses will need staking, honeysuckle tying back . . .
All those wretched sort of jobs will be down to good old Jack!

But her longings, I can see,
increase with sunny weather
so with rule and pen and drawing-board,
we'll work it out together.

Mary-Anne Watson

A GARDENER'S NIGHTMARE
The hedges need trimming, the borders are bare,
Weeds growing like wildfire, and nobody cares.
The roses are rambling right over the door,
Nobody's trimmed them, they're not loved any more.
The lawns need a cutting, the mower won't go,
The pond's a disaster, the fountain won't flow.
The shed is an eyesore, no window or door,
The soil isn't fertile, just chalky and poor.
The fence has the woodworm, it's grotty and brown,
As soon as the wind blows, I know it'll fall down.
The gnomes are quite nasty, they're evil and old,
Their paint's cracked and crumbly, they're covered in mould.
There's snails, ants and greenfly, blackfly and slugs,
Caterpillars, beetles and all kinds of bugs.
The paths are all slippery, the cobbles worn smooth,
I really can't bear it, I'll just have to move!
When all of a sudden, I wake with a fright,
I've just had a nightmare, on what a night!
I rush to the window, what sight will I see,
A garden of beauty, created by me.
Neat lawns and hedges, roses so red,

Nice fences, clean ponds, rich soil, a smart shed.
No slugs or beasties crawling around,
Nice gnomes with faces all smiling, no frowns.
The moral of this tale is simple but clear,
Love your garden and tend it,
lest your nightmare 'comes real.

Sandra Farmer

IDYLLIC GARDENING

Cloudless skies, shimmering leaves,
Look upon weeding as one big yawn
Take advantage of shading trees
No, stay horizontal on the lawn.

Roger Stappleton

SUMMER GARDEN

A walk in my garden
Poses a problem.
Should I drink in the scents
of roses and lavender?
Bend down and breathe
Near carnations and thyme?

Should I sit in my lounger
Under shady straw hat?
Reading letters and magazines
Poems and prose?

Perhaps I should get out
My trowel or spade,
Attacking the cabbage patch
- Turning the earth,
Digging potatoes, picking the peas?
Raking the soil for next year's seeds?

But that which I choose
On a warm summer day
Is to sit with my spinning wheel
Treadling away.
Soaking up sunshine
And green summer scents.
Working the warmth into each
Tiny strand. So the jumper
I wear will be sunny and warm
Bringing memories of summer
In winter's raw blast.

Alison Newbould

REFLECTIONS

The Good Life appealed to me
With produce all home grown
I pictured myself tending
The seedlings I had sown.
I saw French beans a-growing
And beetroot firm and red
Tidy rows of lettuces
All coming to a head;
Green and healthy vegetables
I saw them all take root:
Blossom filled the April sky,
Then luscious ripened fruit.

But I was just a novice
My story must be told
In truth it was a nightmare
Of bugs and slugs tenfold.
On every leaf emerging
To see the light of day
A furry little green thing
Emerged with it to play.
They played upon my cabbage
And burrowed little holes
They dived among the lettuce
And up the French bean poles.

I know there must be experts
Who have all this in hand
For whom the garden produce
Goes just the way its planned,
But if you are a failure -
Green fingers aren't your style,
I'll see you in the market
And sympathise awhile.

Patti Hinsull

EVEN GARDENERS GET FED UP SOMETIMES

So shall I come with spade and line and dreams
To build a garden fit for such as she,
With lion-headed fountains tumbling streams
Of light on scallop shells of porphyry?
A thousand roses I will plant for her,
To scale the walls and catch, with their caresses,
Strands of her scented hair each time she passes.

I'll build a pool with bright reflections there,
Train trim espaliers to lead the eye
On to a bronze, ethereal as air,

As though half poised between brown earth and sky;
A sinuous green dancer, unalloyed
To tactile loam or insubstantial space,
A love-child of the genius of the place.

Tall hanging woods there'll be, to crown each ridge
And give nobility to streams that leap
Cascades and serpentine beneath a bridge,
Then sensually twist and curl through deep,
Still pools of lilies - the hell I will!
God rot her garden and her lily bed:
Today, tell her, I've gone to fish instead.

JamesNash

HAPPY HOLIDAY

Dear John - I feel I should report
on all the things the plants have caught
while you have been in Spain.
There's capsid bugs and slugs and thrips
and all the leaves have yellow tips.
(Could that be acid rain?)

The greenback and the chocolate spot,
though colourful, of course, are not
exactly crop enhancing.
Indeed, it's not a pretty sight;
and rabbits now are every night
relentlessly advancing.
The mildewed leaves fall from the trees
upon the spuds with wart disease.
The lettuces are bolting.
Fusarium wilting of the beans,
combined with blackleg, means the scene's
quite utterly revolting.

Tonight the forecast is hard frost,
but don't despair, all is not lost.
Enjoy the Costa Blanca!
Relax, unwind, don't build up tension,
there's no need for apprehension -
it *might* not be root canker.

You've really earned your holiday,
so just have fun - and, by the way,
I'm filled with admiration,
'cos I've never seen another lawn
with grass that isn't green but fawn -
a brilliant innovation!

It does you good to get away
so why don't you extend your stay -
a fortnight, any how?
Meanwhile, I'll wield flame-gun and spray
and, hopefully, hold all at bay.
So, cheerio for now.

Desmond LePard

LIMERICK

To some there's no hobby like gardening
Organic, synthetic its gladdening
It's ecologically sound
And saves you a pound
But late frost is sheer bloody maddening.

M Humphreys

UNTITLED

As a garden boy
Armed with wheelbarrow, brush and shovel
I swept up after others.
In between the menial tasks
I learned about the nature of plants,
Was taught the art of seed sowing, of taking cuttings.
Experienced the thrill of the first signs of germination,
Of cuttings taking root.
Realised that I had not given new life
Only provided the right conditions.
Forty five years on
Armed with wheelbarrow, brush and shovel
I sweep up after myself,
Sow seeds, take cuttings.
Anxiously await that moment when seeds germinate
And cuttings root.
And when they do I experience that same thrill,
Marvel at the wonder of nature and the Creator of life,
As I did as a garden boy.

David A Garside

UNTOUCHABLE SUN

Rising quietly, almost shy,
Soothing sun in eastern sky,
Emerald velvet covered in dew,
Shimmering crystals calming so new.

Radiant warm, inspiring healing,
Flora like gem's dancing appealing,
Soft blue skies caressing breeze,
Golden silence, still at ease.

Sun of amber closing the day,
Reflecting clouds pink and grey,
Serenely sadly losing height,
Mysteriously hiding through the night.

Mariza Arnold

PERENNIAL PEST

You may bemoan your aphids
Of greenfly you despair
And the sight of circling whitefly
may make you tear your hair

I can cope with all these problems
For each there is a cure
I fearlessly fight these little hordes
and still have strength for more

The pest which stalks my garden
Does damage on a scale
that leaves me in desperation
As all my efforts fail

My bulbs are eaten as they emerge
all eager to flower for me
No chance do they have in my garden
my pest eats those for tea

My seedlings he has for afters
Those he cannot eat he spoils
The sight of him sets me screaming
and sets my blood to boil

No sapling bark is safe from him
Nor pansies in their pot
My nut eating pest the squirrel
... sweet and charming he is not.

Dora Roberts

TRANSFORMATIONS

Autumn cherry blushes ephemerally,
Veiled, impressionistic, finger art,
Spatially perfected.
Pink on a brown background
Shimmers through January,
A winter bride, blossoms fall on the muddied turf.
But this intensely, pregnant lady,
Epitome of promise,
Dwindles to a spindly matron
Incongruously green and wasted.

Actinidia kolomikta; gnarled,
Dormant with nuggets of twisted fingers,
Tenuous, brown and fragile,
Hovering between life and death.
A summer transfiguration;
Tissue-green leaves, paint-pot dipped, tie-dyed,
Pink and white exotica, erotic leaves patterned,
Swilled full of colour;
Up the trellis struts a fretted mannequin.

Valerie Hockaday

ADIEU MY OLD COTTAGE GARDEN

Here it begins . . .
when Shakespeare died
and timber beams were trussed
and someone settled . . .

Well start here . . .
With the soil I've turned
a thousand times (it seems)
nurturing still the genes
of Tudor life and the aeons
of neighbouring Bricksbury Hill.

The garden has no eglantine,
no bank on which the wild thyme blows,
no oxlips;
but the sweet musk-rose
and nodding violets here are yet
with never can each spring forget -
me-not the rampant clematis
o'er-looking seals of Solomon
and hazel witches, lily fronds,
wisteria and the lilac blooms . . .
e'en honeysuckle 'round the door;
scent in the air of lavender.

Columbine, rosemary, marjoram,
wood sorrel, bluebell, anemone, all
conjoin to predispose my mind
towards those glorious sunny days
the pastoral dreams of yesteryear.

No speedwell, rain or binding weed,
no fog or nettle, raging storm
shall mar this verdure, this Elysium.

Eric Smart

AUTUMN BEGINNINGS

I felt the slightest cold creep off the earth,
As tending slackened stems, and faded flowers
Now falling in their autumn sloth,
Chill hovered, reminder of a winter's power,
Staid and still, the waters slowing pace,
Now clear, translucent browns, replace the sun's
Light, subdued and lowly, flows this place
Those busy days of teeming life have run,
thinning, quiet trees, leaves large and darkened greens
Now tinging yellows, as the sap seeps down,
To rest, renewed in peaceful sleep, unseen
Continual cycle, toils beneath the ground,
As autumn begins.

Homer

AUTUMN

The old clock measures the passing of time.
Echoing around the silent room, once so cluttered now cleared,
it's tick tock, tick tock, tick tock,
passes out through the open window to mingle pleasantly
with the evening's sounds.

With the promise of spring fulfilled
peace is descending on our garden.
Here among the last glorious expressions of creation,
the hushed falling of autumn's leaves,
the muffled scent of autumn's last flowers,
is the realisation of all that we have had,
given to us and won by our efforts.

So we stand, you and I, unafraid.
Happy to have played a part,
to have reached this point.

Standing underneath this aged apple tree,
its boughs unburdened from a load
which now lays scattered and mouldering
about our feet, visited only by the occasional wasp
whose wings add strangely to the peace.

So as we move,
you and I,
out to the garden's edge,
let us remember
what we have been.
And as the last glow
of the burnished sun
is replaced by the silver light,
let us embrace,
you and I.

Russell T Martin

THE SEEDLING
Microcosm of life
Burning with ambition
On an earthen stage,
Roots emerging,
Seed leaves praying
Hands together.
Then, without applause
The star accepts its accolade
With opened arms.

Diane Sinclair

BRIEF ENCOUNTER

Slips against the sucking roots,
Guided by a vision
Blind,
Upwards! he must press
The slick loops of flesh.

Headless, legless strand of life,
That plunges through the sharpened
Air,
Knots around the trodden leaf
Sinking slowly back beneath.

And see the shine of the weapon
As the man with love-stained
Fingers
And affection scars the soil,
Feeding his paradise with toil.

He here impels his world to fruit
In this portion of his
Planet,
Pinches together the infinite round,
His blood-tinged helper from below the ground.

A gardener of the light
Meets a gardener of the
Depths,
Now side by side their earth surveyed
A moment shared in the evening shade.

Alexandra McKenna

GARDENING GROANS

I ask you horticulturists' pardon
When I say I hate to garden
Pulling weeds or pruning a rose
Really just gets up my nose
All the flowers that I need see
I can watch on my TV.
So why should I spend hours on weeding
When TV Times I could be reading
But sadly for me my sedentary life
Does not enamour my dear wife
For she who has to be obeyed
Keeps hounding me with fork and spade
And she can really test my metal
As with a face like a bulldog chewing a nettle
She shouts at me 'Switch off these telly's
And grab a fork and don your wellies'
While I would rather make some soup
She has me spreading cattle poop
Or tying up old berry canes
In force nine gales or pouring rains
I oft ask 'Lord why can't she see
That cutting grass is not for me'
If I've to prick out much more daisies
I'll end up inside with the other crazies
This gardening larks not half the fun
Of chasing geese with dog and gun
So someone please tell my dear spouse
I'll do all odd jobs inside the house
But if she wants a garden blooming with health
She can do the bloody thing herself.

Brian Field

CAROUSEL

Hammamelis and
Viburnum bodnantense,
Fragrant through blizzard
and Northern blasts.
Snowdrops
prunus and narcissus,
celebrate spring
with perfumed aura
of syringa.
The summer chorus line
of fat peonies,
and scented roses
intoxicate
our senses. Soul
satisfying fare.
Chrysanthemums,
Aster amellus,
bee murmurous nocturne
to autumn's knell.
Brown leaves bestrew
the grass.
The blood-red holly and
the Christmas rose
foreshadow
clamourous bells and
the twin-headed god.

The carousel
whirls the seasons
ever faster
'round the year.

Joan Evans

SWEET CHERRY

Your silken blossoms, pink blushed, kiss the ground
Washed and caressed by silver drops of rain,
Bowed down by darkened skies you cheer our way,
A fitting graceful tribute to a leaden day.

But when the sun shines and again you lift your head
I stand beneath your flowerets gazing up
Into a skein of colour - finding my soul is fed.

The blackbird bobs beneath your laden boughs
His blackened plumes a contrast to your rosy tints,
And many a lover must have made his vows,
As through the mass of petalled heads the sunlight glints.

Sweet tree you shed in delicate showers those shaded heads,
And leave behind a canopy of green,
The weeping rain is still, and spring with summer weds,
and promise of a new found day is seen.

But you will come again into your own
When next the seasons change its dress,
And nature's calendar, so well renowned,
Will once again, the grass caress.

Wilhimina Gwillim

THE GARDENER

In weather fine he may be seen
Content at toil in garden green
Where can be found all nature's wealth
Invested rich within the earth
In pots his fingers ever pressing
Precious promise of life caressing

A miracle from each bursting seed
The beauty born in every weed
This vision of splendour laid on the land
Reward for love and laboured hand.

Margaret Paterson

THE WATERING CAN

A watering can: I am very unhappy,
I seem to be of little use.
So popular once now I'm left in the tool shed,
I've just fallen into disuse.

The gardener here thinks he's ever so clever;
He ordered a hosepipe device
Which goes in the ground, and the water's delivered
In constant supply - at a price!

So here I am sitting in such isolation,
I'm not to be called on it seems.
It's very frustrating when people ignore me -
But I'll put a stop to their schemes.

The radio put out a warning this morning
That hosepipes are banned from today.
And guess who came looking for me in a hurry?
There's no time for him to delay.

So now I am happily being of service.
The gardener thinks it no fun -
His arms are so tired with lifting my weight,
His evening with feet-up has won.

Aileen North

GARDEN SOLACE

I lie awake at night and fret,
Problems, worries, pain and debt.
The dawn arises, no friend to me,
Then a robin sings in a nearby tree.

Down below my garden glimmers pale,
On the wall a nest-box on a nail.
Two busy birds fly to and fro
Feeding their young who hunger so.

As the sun now warms the scene,
My eyes grow used to shades of green,
All different, all part of same,
Parts of plants with a million names.

I see the rock-rose waking now,
Pretty and pure but fleeting though.
The roses greet the sun with gladness,
And now my heart is free of sadness.

The garden calls me and I go,
To trim and prune and reap and sow.
I fell the peace that closes round me.
I feel release from woes that bound me.

I feel the God that made this earth
Take my hand and give re-birth.
I touch the leaves and smell the flowers,
And time dissolves - no more hours.

My wakeful problems were not so bad,
The night oppressed and made me sad.
Here in my own small plot of land
I am Queen and all is grand.

Brenda Larkin

REQUIEM FOR SPRING OR THE FLOWER MUGGER

The earth was hard and cold with frost,
But 'neath the silver birch,
Eager bulbs of narcissi thrust.
The tree their sheltering church.

As Easter came they grew to buds
With promise of life anew,
Growing in gloom all these months
Now a joy for all to view.

They bowed to the hail,
They beamed in the sun,
How could they know their fate?
Like Christ their span of life not run.

An idle boy with bat came by,
His hair as fair as they,
He slashed them down without a sigh,
Now crumpled and crushed lie they!

June Keal

PILGRIM OF THE YEAR TO COME

Fallow fields of January
Lie beneath the virgin snow;
The bitter chill of February
When summer was so long ago.
Then the March winds blow around us
From the north like frozen thorns,
But frost is cleared by April showers
As the Pilgrim of the Springtime dawns.

Blossoms' sweet perfume in May,
Azaleas bloom and roses grow.
The majesty of June's displaying
All of Mother Nature's show.
Then in July we may regret
The passing of Midsummer's Day
But August is ablaze with fire
As the Pilgrim passes on his way.

Cool September is a warning;
Of the autumn she'll foretell,
But one fine October morning
Summer bids a last farewell.
Tired November leaves are falling
Carpeting my garden gold.
Now December night is calling
For the Pilgrim has grown old.

Once again those fields lie fallow
With raindrops beating like a drum,
When Auld Lang Syne will stand to welcome
The Pilgrim of the Year to Come.

Roger Mansbridge

JACK'S DELIGHT

It started as a tiny seed within a little pot,
I put them out and all but this, the frost had got the lot.
I nurtured it with care and love and watched it slowly grow,
I'd lost the packet, so what it was I really didn't know.

It struggled at first but with my help, began to win the fight,
Grew daily stronger reaching high and up toward the light.
When third set of true leaves appeared with no more fear of frost,
I set it out and fed it well regardless of the cost.

Three foot high and still it grew to four five six and seven,
It really was enormous now reaching up to heaven.
Its girth was wide and leaves were broad its sap was very sour,
and even though I pampered it, I never got a flower.

It hid the fence, grew over paths and covered up the shed,
Killed all the plants around its roots, there was an empty bed.
A harbour now for snails and slugs that ate up all my greens,
And left me with no veg at all, they even took my beans.

So when it reached up to the clouds and disappeared above,
With pruners spade and garden fork and hand within a glove,
I ventured out to cut it down and throw it out for good,
but there appeared a golden egg exactly where I stood.

The golden goose had laid it there I'm sure from way up high,
a fortune would descend on me, falling from the sky,
I'm glad I sold that cow of mine although her milk was good,
I think I'd better wake up now, I really think I should.

Back to reality and with a bump return to earth I must,
And in the force of nature I will only put my trust,
And get my just reward from growing shrubs and veg and flowers,
To take delight producing, and the occasional summer showers.

Sylvia Dunn

A GARDEN VERSE

God gifted man a garden his wonders to enjoy
Dewdrops glistening on a rose a new morn's tears of joy
Sweet fragrance of a flower in bloom the songbird's tuneful note
A paradise of bliss and rest a peace that can't be bought.

James McMillan

MY GARDEN

The garden was a haven
Nothing touched for years
My eye's roamed 'round this wilderness
With tall couch grass and briers

There were flowers in every border
Struggling to get though
And tumbling down the old stone wall
Aubrieta, mauves and blue

I saw a cloud of blossom
On the knarled old apple tree
A blackbird sitting at the top
Was singing merrily

I know there will be lots of work
With little time for rest
And I have a strong suspicion
This moment will be best.

Joyce Clifford

POPPADUMS AND MARIGOLDS

Poppadums and marigolds,
Signs for *stop* and *enter*,
Garden gloves and strawberry jam,
You'll find at the garden centre.

Ceramic chimes and *Slug-u-Kill*,
Birthday cards and snax.
Peat and mulch and coco-shells,
Sweets, in handy packs.

Daffodils and wellie boots,
Pot pourri sweetly smelling,
The mind begins to boggle now
Just what they'll next be selling!

To get us parting with our cash
They anticipate most needs.
But *I've* been here ninety minutes now -
And *still* not found the *seeds!*

Barbara Johnson

BACKYARD HOTEL

Small birds play hopscotch on the slabs
drawing my attention to the many guests
who pop into my garden patch.

Thingmies nod brightly, thingies wink,
while snoozing in the shade is that big
something-or-other that looks like furry snakes.

Small green stuff cuddles up beside tall
what-d'ye-call-'ems draped with pretty yellow
blooms, there beside the thingamibob.

Red what's-its-name grows strong and straight
forming an umbrella to keep the sun off
those little blue-tipped petal things.

Beside the wall, in single tubs,
je-ne-sais-quoi's stand with noses in the air,
preferring always separate beds.

They all are welcome, weeds or not.
Some come back here every year. I only wish
I could remember all their names!

Val Pöhler

DISILLUSIONED

A town bred child
No garden had I,
No knowledge of flowers,
Living four floors high.

A thing of wonder
Was a dandelion seed,
A magical fairy
To be trapped and freed.

To be cupped in one's hands
While a wish was made,
Then gently blown upwards
While we silently prayed.

Now I live in the suburbs,
A garden I own,
My knowledge of flowers
Gives me reason to moan.

For now I curse,
As I hoe and I weed,
At the gossamer flight
Of the dandelion seed.

Susan Chevalier

GARDENING

In winter, when the ground lies bare
I garden from my fireside chair.
I browse through catalogues and scheme
To plant the garden of my dreams.

The first weak rays of springtime sun
Reveal a resurrection come
And tempt me out to weed and hoe
Where snowdrops and narcissus grow.

The lengthening days bring blossom trees,
Humming with pollen-drowsy bees.
Now is the time to sow the seed
For every vegetable we need.

Summer's sweet roses bloom and blush,
And fruit hangs ripe on every bush.
Each evening with my watering can
I overcome the hosepipe ban.

Apples and berries, beans and peas,
I pick and bottle, blanch and freeze,
Working from dawn to dusk to save
What nature's generous bounty gave.

At last my harvest's all in store.
The ground lies bare and brown once more.
Resting, renewing, as it lies
Beneath December's wintry skies.

Joan Ungemuth

THE HISTORY OF THE ROSE

We are told it all started with Rose canina,
That dainty dog rose of hedgerows and braes.
Or was it the Romans, or was it the Turks
Or Rosa Chinensis, the red rose of China

Complicata there was, a Gallica rose,
Red rose of Lancaster, white of York,
Gallica Violacea as old as old as they say,
And sweet Rosa mundi that Henry II chose.

Centifolias appeared with one hundred petals,
And delicate scent like the Rose of Provence.
Cabbages were they called, must be the shape,
And the lettuce - leaved rose with pale waxy sepals.

There were Albas and Bourbons, and Portland Rose too,
Celestial, Boule de Neige, Fulgens to name but a few.
Omar Khayyam grew strong on a grave
And Blush Damask there was of pale, pink hue.

HP's took their place in Victoria's reign,
High centred and double, or blowsy and single.
Strong growing Rugosas with large showy hips,
And tea scented roses. From China they came.

Polyanthus and Floribundas with flowers in large clusters,
Jenny Wren, dark Dusky Maiden and Little White Pet.
Scramblers and ramblers, and climbing roses too,
Rambling Rector cascades like white feather dusters.

Last came the new shrubs, by Austin we learn.
Repeat flowering are they and gorgeous the scent.
Lovely Graham Thomas, G Jekyll and Fisherman's Friend.
Oh! glorious rose. Many Happy Returns.

Jean Avery Wright

A PARADISE

I was taken to Valley Gardens, and what did I see
Vistas of Rhododendrons and Azaleas, such beauty
Majestic trees of Silver Birch, Spanish Chestnut and Pine
Don't anyone say there is no God - this was supreme, divine

All the colours of the rainbow were in this panoramic view
In breathtaking wonder I thought - oh this is too lovely to
                                                        really be true
The breeze whispering tenderly, birds singing a hymn to the sun
Complete ecstasy is when God, Spirit and I unite as one

How can I ever forget going for this special treat
We walked together happily admiring the flowers at our feet
The azure space above us, it was the perfect skyline
All this glory and perfection was free, and it was mine

Thank you friend for thinking of me, for giving me a thought
Rare and utter beauty such as this could never ever be bought
Another miracle I saw was a butterfly embracing a flower, a kiss
This beautiful panorama, I will ever remember, sheer bliss.

Doris Bowden

A LATE CONVERSION

There were splendid plants a-plenty in the Gardens of The Trust,
And my horticultural needs were very small,
So I took my little knife, on each outing with my wife,
When we went to view the splendours of some Hall.
I knew it would awful if great hordes of the unlawful
Descended on the Gardens of the land,
Kidnapping plants galore, that I really would deplore,
But there was only me - you understand!

Oh, the shrubs they were a vision of delight and joy to me,
As we marvelled at the borders in the grounds.
Like a busy little bee, I snipped lots of cuttings free,
And my garden did improve, by leaps and bounds!
I've *Clytaemnestra Burgeonalis,* a unique and lovely rose,
And along this wall, a wonderful display
Of *Clematis Spiritatis,* and my very, very latest,
An endangered species from a Castle in Moray!

I was taken quite aback, when someone said the other day,
That the Trust is now employing private eyes,
Who patrol their lovely grounds, like botanical bloodhounds,
And spell the amateur collector's sad demise.
It really is quite awful, but it seems that hordes unlawful
Have preyed upon the Gardens of the land,
And purloined each blooming shoot, and each ripened seed and root,
And it wasn't only me . . . I understand.

Jenny Ogilvie

A GARDENER GROWS OLD

Turn back the compost heap of life,
And find green thoughts, still grassy and entire,
And memories, with rainbow petals pinched by time.

Spread wide the slow manure of work
Which, well placed, turns dross to gold;
And toss aside all bitter thoughts
Eaten through by worms of mind,
Too hard, too prickly to be absorbed.

And then at last, find under all
A seam of life's decayed events,
Rich to mulch the autumn's glory.

Robin Robbins

THE JOYS OF GARDENING

When to the country I removed,
My face lit up with glee
At the thought of having land,
A gardener, I would be.

My thoughts were full of plants and shrubs,
Of colour schemes and ponds,
Of lazy days spent on my deck chair
Eating strawberries and cream.

I had expected aphids, slugs and snails,
Blackspot, rust and mites,
Even mildew, lice and virus
Had not failed to cross my mind, but,

The heron's eaten all my fish,
The pheasant's scratched up turf,
Wrens are nesting in my baskets
And mice have done their worst.

The squirrels do just as they please,
And rabbits damage even trees!
As for moles, they've joined me too,
I just don't know what I can do.

I really long for my old back yard,
Covered in concrete slabs,
For the peace I found between those walls
In that plant and pest free patch!

Caroline Merrington

GARDEN IN WINTER

Winter.
The dead months.
Grey soil, cracked
Beneath
Trees brown and bare.
Earth gripped fast
In the vice of death:
A corpse awaiting its burial.

Brave leaves
Patter uneasily,
Daring to shake
Then clap their hands
In the wind of a worn-out winter.
Eerie applause
Welcoming snow from the gravid cloud.

Slowly,
Spiralling,
The soft flakes fall:
Smothering soft the cruel, cruel thorn;
Hushing the rattle of leaves;
Embracing the tired and torn;
Embalming the ground
With a soft-down,
Soft-down shroud.

Ann Rawson

GNOMOPHOBIA

I hate those little garden gnomes
Who only stand and stare.
With evil eyes and upturned noses
They guard the sweet peas and the roses.

The captain of my neighbour's lot
Stands fishing in the onion plot
With rod erect, I do suspect
Subversive action from the clot.

They've frightened all my birds away.
They frighten me, I have to say.
My friends all know I hate them so
And hide their gnomes until I go.

But Mum and Dad, God bless their souls,
Brought me a present from their hols.
You've guessed, of course, it's one of those,
A nasty gnome in stupid pose.

I just wish that someone would kill him stone dead
Then I could sleep easy in my bed.
Maybe some poison would do the trick,
Or should I bash him with a great heavy brick?

I could sink the hatchet in his smug little head,
And bury him deep in a hole under the shed.
Murder most wicked is my object today,
If I think carefully I might make it pay.

Dead Gnomes Incorporated I will become
'Cos I'll get no peace till the fould deed is done.
There must be others who think as I do,
Free gardens for people - that means me and you.

Valerie Edge

MY GARDEN

In spring there are daffodils gleaming,
With primroses shining yellow.
Blossoms bedecking the trees,
And birds building nests in the hollow.

In summer the roses are blooming,
Sweet peas fragrance the air.
The honeysuckle, herbs hum with bees,
And for one day the peonies flare.

In autumn the trees bow their heads,
Laden with ripening fruit.
Nectarine, apple, plum, pear,
All hanging there, full, round and sweet.

In winter all's peaceful and quiet,
The flowers and the trees take their rest,
The birds come to feed at the table,
And the brown earth sleeps.

Jean Hillier

SPANISH GARDEN

As I balance between
Green lines of beans
Hoeing the persistent weeds
That cling to the steep sloping soil
The mountains watch closely.

Ranged like curious neighbours
They admire the purple aubergines
And approve the yellow melons
Swelling in their compost rich beds.

At noon the sun scorches my sandalled feet
And I descend to rest in the fig tree shadow
To breathe the scent of lavender and wild peppermint,
While peacock butterflies and pollen dusted bees
Hover like attentive lovers over the white rose.

Now hazy with the midday heat
The mountains gaze impassively
As you cross the crushed thyme grass
And lie in the cool green shade with me.

Mary Ellis

THE ROSE GARDEN

The scent of roses filled the air that lazed across my brow,
While petals streaked with red and pink swayed to the breezes tune.
This tranquil garden so hidden well behind a high topped wall,
Is home for many roses, their names a secret still.
They cling to stone works crumbling edge and fall from every crevice,
They climb and tangle in the trees, and the petals fall like snow,
In every bed a bush or tree, or ramblers take a hold,
Their colours range from white to gold, from red to dark maroon,
Each flower is a different shape, the petals curl and fold,
And every one a miracle of nature's loving hand.
The gardeners of olden times knew much of *how to please*,
They planted roses every where, the owners eyes to tease.
Every corner holds a treat, a flower of delight,
A crimson bud, a golden spray, a mottled growing shower,
Each in its self a work of art, no man could ever capture.
This gardens filled with fragrant blooms, a sanctuary of quiet,
It is a place where time stands still, and only ghosts do walk.

Rosie A Rumble

CONSERVATION

I've got a garden, very green and wide.
It runs right 'round my little house
and down the other side.
It isn't very tidy
and is never free from weeds.

Nettles thrive all summer long
and mingle with my seeds.
I don't think Mr Titchmarsh
would approve my weedy plot,
But, after all, in these green days
Conservation is what I've got.

Emma Barry

SNOWY GARDEN

As the snow falls,
The garden becomes more,
magically white.
The snowdrops fade into the white,
The moon will shine on them tonight,
glistening under stars so bright,
Twinkling shoots frosted solid firm and tight.
Standing still the statue
winks smiling at the whiteness
as it softly gently sinks to the ground.

Laura F Pocock (12)

MY LANDRAKE GARDEN

Summer jasmine, winter heather,
Primrose in all kinds of weather,
Snowdrops, scillas, phlox and more
I grow beside my garden door.

The starlings chase away the finch
But Robin will not give an inch.
Housemartins soaring on the wing
Are heralds of another spring.

Bronze acer with blue sky above,
A canopy I'll always love
But give me for that special thrill
The first bright golden daffodil.

Kay Tompson

BEHIND THE SPADE

Behind the spade I spend my time
Now that I've left the sea.
No tang of salt; instead it's lime
With soils acidity.
No heaving deck beneath my feet,
No spray to lash my face.
I hoe a healthy row of beet
And find it's no disgrace.

Before the mast one fights for life
Against an angry foe,
But that is nought compared to strife
Now that I dig and sow.
The raging wind and crashing wave
With skill is overcome.
Bugs give battle to the grave,
Follow no rule of thumb.

Around the world the sights to see,
From Plymouth Hoe to Perth,
But now the thrill of life for me,
Home produce from the earth.
Fruit, flowers and veg bought from a stall
Leave much to be desired,
My compost heap provides withall
Next season's growth inspired.

Roy E Lewin

BEHIND THE SPADE

Is this how it used to be
Behind the spade for victory?
They dug and sowed and grew and grew
While overhead the Spitfires flew.

Is this how it ought to be
Behind the spade for you and me?
We read the books that tell us when
To plant the seeds, and harvest them.

But books don't tell you what to do
When it rains and rains and freezes too;
And pruning cuts are clearly shown
But none look like the trees we own.

So learn from the tortoise not the hare,
Behind the spade lest you despair
Remember as you hoe and weed, that
Patience grows the finest seed.

Irene Baker

THE UGLY BUG BALL

Slugs and snails and nasty things
Are underneath the ground,
They live their lives as snug as bugs
In slimy little mounds.

They slither out on odd occasions
Just to have a look,
Then chomp their way through treasured plants
and sneak back to their nook.

Inconsiderate of gardeners
they squelch their way through life,
Immune to our distress
on finding *crawlies* running rife.

The garden centre spray
can be a wonderful deterrent,
But principles and love of life
are sadly too inherent.

I'm forced to let them have a ball,
Diversify my sorrow.
The garden, after all,
is just our luxury to borrow.

Jean Roberts

MICHAEL

Here's a cautionary tale about Michael
Who would never, anything, recycle.
    When he up and died
    His wife cried and cried
Then into the compost tossed Michael.

Jane Spray

UNTITLED

Each morning when I arise,
A scene of beauty greets my eyes.
A gift that changes from day to day,
Crocus in February, Tulips in May.
In March the Daffodils bob and sway,
Greeting the day with a golden wave.

Come Summer the Roses and Lilies invite
The onlooker to stroll and sample their delight.
Nature's bed time gift in Autumn arrives,
Maple and Rowan brighten dull skies.
With Winter's frost on a garden at rest,
I can ask for no more, I have the best.

Lynn Nash

THE GARDEN - A SONNET ON IT

So now the year its cycle turns again,
And shoots from 'neath the earth begin to show.
In spite of hailstones, frost, or fill-dyke rain
Old nature gives the green light, saying 'Go!'
And so, with feet encased in wellies green,
The gardener, and his spouse also, no doubt,
Will start their labours, eager, joyful, keen
To see the early signs of spring break out:
Those little spears of tender green that rise
Through hardest soil, or in the cracks between
The stones or pebbles which, 'neath winter skies,
Were all that longing eyes had, waiting, seen:
But now, with spring, our hearts within us boil,
Exhorting us to start anew our loving toil.

Ian W Millar

TO A CABBAGE

A cabbage now, the housewife who
Stays home to guard the growing brood,
Do all the housework and prepare the food
As old-time mothers used to do.
A cabbage now, according to career wives
Who follow free their private lives

Not the slim, trim form of the swaying sweet pea.
More the figure, only bigger, of the buxom peony.
Not the perfume to the nose as the lily or the rose.
Nor the passion to the lip as the cider-apple sip.
So whatever is the balm for your universal charm?

Like sophisticated ladies of the stage and screen
The flowers with fleeting glamour decorate the scene.
They titillate the fancy and tantalise the mind,
But yours is a splendour of a different kind,
Transient beauty leaves the face,
Constant heart preserves the grace.

With us throughout every season
For us, never mind the reason.
In our love and lust for living,
We consume completely all your giving.
It is for us you live your life,

Dear cabbage, dear wife.

Trevor Williams

CALL OF THE WILD

Testily tending my urbanised cottage
Garden
The soothing country sounds of bovine lowly moo-ing
And plaintive baa-ing of sheep
safely grazing
Assail my ears from the nearby slopes
Of *tidy* surrounding hills
Why?
I sadly meditate and cogitate
Do I spend long hours of toil
Tilling my light sandy soil

Applying man-made chemicals
To my man-made minute *lawn*
(smothering an involuntary yawn)
When
Out there all is peacefully
Breathtakingly and beautifully *tidy!*
But answer comes there none
And days' work's just begun -
Ain't *nature* marvellous!

Peter H Adams

AND THEN GREEN LIGHT

Winter is actually
The thorn squashed and strangled
The leaf dried
With a cold hand trailing

Stories of sleep.

Winter is an urgent but sure argumentor,
A wet orb that lingers a little too long.
A dead silent look
Upon the face of a loved one.

The seasonal festivities
That parade this season
Of the death-mask,
Are a vain attempt to ignore
The true passage
And tale forgotten.

To the basic eye feeling,
Winter is dry-eyed death
Coming blue and grey touches
Colour storms hatching

Monochromatic rain.

Martin Paul Smith

EXPLANATION PLEASE?

I know why
Hippopotami
Like *mud!*
It cooools their blood:
They go down to the hollow,

But, this I can't follow -

No joke
Some folk
Love to *walla*
In Squalla!

Minna Rickaby

THE FLOWER'S LOST BLOOM

So sad the petals when falling down,
The flower discarding her glorious crown.
Like offspring expelled awaiting their doom,
A mother alone, the flower's lost bloom,
Like teardrops they fall to colour the ground.
The purple, the yellow, the blue and the brown,
The orphans of nature just waiting to die,
Just blowing around, as we tread them goodbye.
Rita Morgan

MISS BONNER BAKES BREAD

Miss Bonner began to be bothered
by things that they put in her food.
She worried about the E numbers
and the poisons and pesticides used;
She'd heard all these colours and chemicals
could alter the course of her moods.

So she started soaking her lentils
and doing strange things with brown beans.
Her compost burned with excitement,
as she ate her organic greens.
She felt the vegan enlightenment
of your food being just as it seems.

Miss Bonner began to be bored,
while one day kneading brown bread,
she saw the petals of her poppies had fallen,
and seed pods had formed there instead.
Loaves scattered with seeds look attractive,
'I'll try those on my baking' she said.

Miss Bonner felt strange and peculiar;
dandelions grew in her head,
her ears needed constantly weeding,
the lawn on her face to be fed.

Advice on the slugs in her nostrils
she found quite difficult to find,
but the snails who crawled on her tonsils
were almost invariably - kind.

Rebecca Farmer

THE WILDERNESS

There was a garden here once,
Now bind weed and leggy bramble grow
And hog weed, head high, spills its seeds
On untilled border soil below.

The gardeners lived here once;
Within a bothy of stone that yet still stands.
But the roof lies mangled within the stonework
And nettles invade the neighbouring land.

There were pathways here once
That footfalls and barrows rutted with sound;
No gardener now checks the onslaught of bramble
Casting ever deep shade over gravel and ground.

There is a wilderness growing here now,
That nature, untamed, will continue to sow,
Gently erasing the borders and hot beds
Until the land once again feels the cut of the hoe.

Brian L Giggins

PEST ASIDE

Snail after snail
Went into the pail
Slug upon slug
Went into the trug
Did he whisper, 'I beg your pardon,'
As he tossed them into next door's garden?

Cavan Syrad

LABOUR IN VAIN

Behind the spade I sweat and toil,
To create a beauty from the soil.
I hoe, and rake, dress and feed,
Make a tilth to sow the seed.
And when the shoots begin to show
I feel so proud of what I grow.

Then the aphids, thrips and grubs
Descend on flowers, trees and shrubs.
The birds they all come down to feed,
They steal my newly sown grass seed.
They peck at buds and sometimes flowers
And spoil the work of hours and hours.
The squirrel comes to chew the nut
And stays to dig the crocus up,
He nibbles a bit and leaves the rest;
That squirrel has become a pest!

It's all hard work with little to show
Through the wind, the rain and snow.
I'll concrete it over and paint it green,
And once a week sweep it clean.

But in summer when visitors call
You take them 'round and show them all.
And say with pride upon the spot,
'It's all my work, this blooming plot!'

R P Tonks

Worm Warning

Take care my child and do not goad
The Annelid or Nematode
Lumbricus (common worm to you)
Takes in the Platyhelminth too;

But there is something you should learn
Even the common worm can turn.
The Platyhelminth may decide
To take up home in your inside;
Once in this comfortable abode
He may invite the Nematode.
Heed this advice, you may have heard
The worm is for the early bird!

Jack Rowe

BEES ON ECHINOPS

Have you ever seen a bee,
In a drunken stupor lay?
Far too dozed and dopey,
To move or fly away.

Watch them on the echinops
So full of nectar sweet,
With baggy pants of pollen
Around their legs and feet.

When it comes to evening,
The sun has set and gone,
Those drowsy little creatures,
Are too sleepy to fly on.

They take their bed and breakfast there,
Of life there is no sign,
Like old men made quite tipsy,
On potent home-made wine.

And when they have recovered,
Their work begins anew,
Producing pounds of honey,
Enjoyed by me and you.

Joy Ginger

THE DARKBORN

Blow gentle breeze all drifting clouds speed by,
Shine forth o'Sun, add nourish to
The shrunken frame of earth that we
Might glean the energy from warming soil
To push our budding tips into nature's air,
And fill the land with flowers of spring.

Gordon Litchfield

BEHIND THE SPADE

We have such dreams us gardeners,
It's all inside our head
Waiting for that day to come
When spring says go ahead,
Then one day you look around
and things are on their way
The daffodils are nodding as if
they want to say,
'Look at me I'm here again,
dancing for your pleasure,
until it's time for me to go,
and make way for another.'
Clematis and roses are entangled
in delight,

Lupins-delphiniums-hollyhock
all towering proud and bright,
patio pots full of life bursting
at the seams,
Let's not forget the cabbage
white and all of those species,
Now some blooms are fading
Autumn's on its way,
It's been a lovely summer,
and what more can I say
We've all enjoyed the garden
eating, sitting and play,
But I'm the workforce in our garden,
I'm behind the spade.

Joan Bradshaw

LEAVES

In autumn,
my father swept up leaves
with an unforgiving curse and ferocity
that made me think they were the sky falling.

He swept them
so relentlessly, as if
each fall was like another leaf
torn out from his ever-short book of life.

The brush moved without compromise,
grating against both concrete and grass,
And while neighbours let leaves sit and rot,
my father saw it best to get rid.

He saw them as trespassers,
souls who blocked drains, made paths slippery.
But another force kept him sweeping;
more autumn as destructive force.

I told him.
I thought the task was worthless.
'Let it happen, sit and relax,' but he could not.
Those leaves were his grey hairs, his bald spot.

And as he swept,
he thought of China, Venice and other places
he wished he might have travelled to,
but instead came home from work to curse.

In doing all this
my father banned autumn.
A word not spoken, a time not needed.
He knew what he was doing.

'Let the leaves settle,'
his brow spoke to me, 'and you settle with them,'
And so I watch to see the day he stops,
when he shall pass me the leaf-brush.

Alan M Kent

PARADISE

It's only twelve yards square - my patch
of glorious English soil
And every inch is tilled with love
Not sweat and tears and toil.

In spring the bluebells call me out
and the daffodils stand proud
The crimson tulips hold their heads
high over the forget-me-not cloud.

When summer comes the days are warm
the mornings wet with dew.
That's fallen on my garden friends
of red and yellow and blue.

The blackbird wakes me with a song
perched high in my apple tree
and in the lilac the thrush's call
'I'm free - I'm free - I'm free.'

Shelagh Stannard

MIRACLES

My garden is a truly beautiful thing
Giving me pleasure from winter to spring,
Then following through into summer's bright glow
And onward to autumn's soft mellowing show.

My garden's so peaceful, a haven of rest,
From the day's careworn toil with its silence I'm blessed.
Isn't it wondrous the shapes I can see
In bushes and flowers so diverse, flowing, free?

The birds come to visit, tuck into the feast,
Share insects and berries, though these aren't the least
Of wildlife to come; grubs and beetles, fat toads
Striped wasps, busy ants and bees with heavy loads
Of pollen for honey, their buzzing will lull
And send me to sleep in the sun - then a gull
Will swoop from above with its loud raucous cry
To tell me the year is fast passing me by.

Then sadly the days start to draw in and soon
My garden will mostly be lit by the moon,
So planning in armchair for spring's early show
Will have to suffice when it's zero below!

But miracles happen again - look green shoots
A snowdrop, bright crocus and more sprouting roots.
Oh! Spring's on the way, time to sow seeds and start
To welcome another year, refresh my heart.

Paddy Jupp

ALL FINENESS AND FINERY GOES TO EARTH

All aglow, aflame, ruby-ruddy, fire and fresh wounds bloody
Revealed colour rich and rosy in the greenling maze
Cells crushed and crumpled, moribund, unveiling
a vivid, colour-crazed, final phase of waning,
dying in a blaze of scarlet glory
a crimson banner briefly blazing beauty
dappled darkly in determined brown decay
shortly feeding foliage finely; in a solid, earthy way.

Clover

BISHOPSWOOD

There is so much life
In this garden of mine,
And it's not only me . . .
When the weather is fine
I'm out with the hoe,
The spade and the fork
Full of plans to dig deep . . .
But I'm tempted to talk
To my gardening neighbour:

And commiserate over
Snail-ridden beans
And lawns covered in clover,
Roses smothered in aphis,
Pigeon devastated crops,
Mole hills everywhere
And peacock nibbled phlox . . .
And yet - I hear the thrush
Beat the snail on stone
And blackbirds are
Busy on the rowan.
In the deep, green moss
On the old stone wall
The restless wrens forage.
In the bright, blue borage
The lively bee works
And the ladybirds crawl
Tirelessly on leaves
Of lemon balm growing tall.
This lively little world -
- Of which I am so fond
Is a mirror, yet happier, -
- than that greater one beyond.

S Bishop

ODE TO THE ANTI-GARDENER

That wild, neglected garden's
hard untended earth
no dearth of pristine daisy
fit for tickling caterpillar chain;
plush meadow-ragged unshorn grass
crushed into unlasting patterns

Barely warmed beneath a sky
as innocently blue
as china-dolly eyes
and infant May's
first rowdy tumbling breeze

That frisks each tender
fresh-clothed leaf
to shimmying serenade
and flings a fragile host
of fairy clocks to scattering
translucent seed

That humble corner's
ragged view,
untrammelled by ornate design,
lies easy in subdued content
begs no relentless sharp-edged tool
to intervene
but leave her fine abandoned patchwork
free
to myriad minute scurryings
and hummings of an ancient harmony.

Shirley Frost

A BLACKBIRD'S SONG

The lady in my garden grows such lovely things to eat,
Currants, raspberries, strawberries, all succulent and sweet;
She does her best to keep me out but hasn't managed yet
For it's really only nestling's play to creep beneath the net!

I suppose it is unethical to use a crafty beak
To steal from one who feeds me when the weather's cold and bleak,
But, after all, I'm just a bird and no one can expect
A feather brain to reason with a human intellect!

J A Bush

GARDEN IN THE DUSK

Come walk with me in the quiet dusk
Where the heady perfumes hang in the air
Of honeysuckle and night-scented-stock
And the fragrance of roses fair.

In the twilight hours the garden sleeps
While a light wind whispers in the trees,
Old are the secrets of the garden flowers
Carried on the warm soft breeze.

Forgotten is the toil at the end of the day,
As the light fades in the gathering dark,
The spirit of the garden is hidden away
Till the rising of the lark.

Marion Robinson

A TREE

A tree is a beautiful sight to behold,
But in the winter when the winds blow cold,
She stands there bare, her leaves all shed
Like a lovely lady preparing for bed,
With the long sleep ahead.
But then, in the spring she bursts forth again,
In her new spring gown.
When the birds will sing, and the sun shines like gold,
A tree is beautiful to behold.

G Sandiford

BLUE

I am given joy by sight of blue
Within the garden as I pass;
A favourite shade that speaks to me
Throughout the year from plot and grass.
I see the borage, shy heads bent,
Bell-bright and vivid as they shake
Their richly-royal robes, as blue
As foreign seas or mountain lake.
With downward look the merry glance
Of flowers diminutive I meet.
Were ever eyes so precious blue
As speedwell waiting at my feet?
Lobelia lingers on the bank
As if unwilling to forgo
The summer days, the kind warm winds,
And beauty they have cherished so.
Others stand with petals dipped
In dyes superb and magical;
Delphiniums stretching up so high,
And Jacob's ladder pitched less tall.
Bluebell and gentian gleam, and I
Must marvel at their brilliant dress.
How came such colour, so intense,
From dark earth-mould to loveliness?
Salute the soil that gives to us
Such miracles at which to stare.
Praise rain and sun; praise precious seed
Entrusted to our human care.

I bless a world wherein I grew
Aware of this delightful blue.

Winifred Corrin

NETTLE RASH

Sent all the way from famous town
The tiny seeds like pollen brown
Would fill my garden summer through
With flowers of every shade and hue.
At least that's what the grower said.
In colourful catalogue I had read!
The very name inspired my trust
Although the seed resembled dust
For *begonia semperflorens* meant
Flowering always, never spent!
Each speck producing gorgeous sight
To fill my heart with pure delight.
Such rapture at their germination
Made greater still determination
To show the world that I could grow
Blooms fit for finest flower show!
With tender care and suitably nourished
My tender begonia plantlets flourished.
Alas hopes dashed to the ground
The day with heavy heart I found
Instead of rainbow coloured petals
I'd grown a lot of stinging nettles
And weal's like *urticarian rash*
Itched to regain my wasted cash!

Roselie Mills

SELF HEAL

There's a healing in a garden,
Whether old, or any grade,
If you grub among the bushes
Or dig with fork or spade.

When your life seems topsy turvey
And your heart is like a stone . . .
Then go pull up weeds from borders,
Or mix up sand with loam.

You'll find your heart *is* lighter,
After pulling up those weeds.
There's a cure somewhere in a garden . . .
Is it found when on our knees?

Doris Beer

A GARDEN

What delight to all is a garden with its secrets beneath the earth,
The magic of every season, the joy of every birth.
Springtime with the daffodils and gentle crocus there -
Hyacinths perfumed sweetly and the tiny snowdrop fair.
Summer brings true glory, the roses reign supreme -
Everything is blooming in nature's glorious scheme.
Sunflowers reaching for the sun luring golden bees,
The many striking greens of all the stately trees -
And grass an emerald carpet, like velvet to the touch -
God's rich earth is giving, a gardens means so much.
Every bed and border shows such loving care,
Each bloom is perfection with beauty that is rare.
Autumn with its mellow sun brings an ever-changing scene -
Like an artist swiftly stealing it gently strokes the green -
Bringing gold and red to dazzle every eye.
The nights grow dim and sunny days seem to hurry by.
Then the frost of winter stretches forth its hand -
All is sparkling bright in this garden wonderland
Snowflakes gently swirling so quietly they fall -
A cloak of gleaming white will quickly cover all.
Beauty all around us completing nature's plan -
A garden surely is one of God's great gifts to man.

Jean Amor

TO A ROSE

Oh beauteous rose of sweetest breath
Beloved in life and mourned at death
When petals shed and we are weeping
Lovely rose is only sleeping
Through warmth of sun and sip of rain
Oh wondrous rose you wake again.

Kathleen Cawley

THE KELSAE ONION

At Christmas they are sown
To grow on a bed, or plot
By September they are grown and shown
To beat them all. Yes! The lot!

Their size! A sight for sore eyes
Capable of winning any prize
They give months of growing pleasure
But the flavour! That's to treasure.

Not only are they good looking
they relish all kinds of cooking
Roasting, stewing, frying, grilling
Super with your favourite filling.

Why not pop them in the microwave
Or eat them raw, then heat you save
The onion bed is a pretty sight
But on a plate they're sheer delight.

They store well all winter through
Until the season starts anew
Where would we be without *Kelsae*
Fun to grow, A treat to eat! I'll say!!

Ian McPherson

THE SECRET GARDEN

I found a secret garden
With a crazy paving path.
It led me to a tiny stream
Where birds could take a bath.

There were violets growing freely
And bluebells by the stream.
Rabbits frolicked in the grass
And the orchids were a dream.

Red and white toadstools
Scattered underneath the trees.
I kept expecting fairies
To appear below my knees.

Ferns were growing in abundance
With lovely feathery fronds,
Frogs were basking on the stones,
As they do in nature's ponds.

I have kept this garden secret,
And trust that you will too.
It's still a secret garden
For I've told no one but you.

Dorothy Bassett

THE GARDEN IN AUTUMN

Today I walked through my garden
on a carpet of colourful leaves.
The beautiful shades of the season
tumbling down on the autumn breeze.

One lovely, last rose of the summer
held its petals now waiting to die.
As shafts of sunlight overhead
filtered down from a cloudless sky.

The songs from the garden birds
echoed through the crisp, cold air.
Soon winter snows would be falling
on the branches now laid bare.

A magical scene surrounded me
on this dry, autumnal day.
The great season of fruitfulness,
God's handiwork there on display.

Honey Wilde

OUTSIDE IN MY GARDEN

Outside, in *my* garden,
I saw the morning dew,
burst-open a prism
of delicious hues.

Here comes a spider,
(there's a fly in *his* prison)
and he spins,
and he spins,
as his mouth
opens wider.

Those black dangly threads
are *his* octave of legs
that creep along silk lines
like musical notes
in movements that crochet
a delicate web.

Now *he* clings to the air
on one quavering chord,
whilst I, swallow the juicy fly
at my own accord.

Mary O'Dwyer

The Gardening Bank
My back cries 'Oh no! He's at it again,'
Digging the garden in the wind and the rain,
Knees will be aching from kneeling on stones,
Sometimes the pain seems to enter the bones,
Everything's done for the gardens needs,
But away for a fortnight - just look at the weeds,
Friends say I'm lucky and always so neat,
Yes that's called hard work I *always* repeat,
It works like a bank - I just want to shout,
'If you put nothing in - then you get *nothing* out!'

A J Perry

MOLLIE'S CLIMBING ROSE

One day soon, I know I will
I'll go out there and move that rose
Planted right, its roots not wet
Plenty of room and plenty of light

But it's not happy, so neither am I
What to do! What to do!

Given by Mollie with much love
I need it not to die!
Should I feed, should I mulch
Should I prune, or should I move
What to do! What to do!

Louise C Evans

GASTROPOD

Slime, slime, slip, slurp,
Wave, weave, slime, slip,
Chomp, chomp, slurp, burp,
Gurgle, burble, slime, slip,
Chomp, wave, chomp, glug,
Hey - ho! I'm a slug - ugh!

Richard Swale

MY SANCTUARY

My garden is of uncommon shape,
It's big and rather rambling,
All year long it gives me joy
And in it I love ambling.
It has a wild and wooded end
Where compost heaps abound,
The shed is hidden down there too,
And a secret hide-out found . .
Then there's a productive side
Along the left hand border,
Where runner beans and strawberries
Climb and spread, in order.
My favourite part, the flower-beds,
Requires endless labour,
To say nothing of the money spent
To stock them full to savour!
There's wildlife in these grounds aplenty,
The foxes slink through nightly,
Birds of different size and species
And squirrels with antics so sprightly!
All in all, the garden is my sanctuary,
Its work and pleasure in one,

I wish I had more time out there,
When all is said and done!

Madeleine McWilliam

DIG FOR VICTORY

Mankind preys upon mankind.
Yet in the garden there is tranquillity.
The seasons change yet are the same
The familiarity of spring following winter
Brings a reassurance that life
Will go on just the same. As always.
In the garden it is safe. Secure.
Man-made reality is shut out.
We can *dig for victory* and in our own
Small but important way help redress the balance,
Try to restore the damage cruel mankind has done.
At least we can make a start.
Hope lies buried in the garden.

Deborah Hearn

AMANUENSIS HONORARIUS
(Private thoughts of the Secretary to a County Gardens Trust)

Names indecipherable,
Meetings interminable,
papers innumerable,
   Failing Hon. Sec.
Proposals unfathomable,
Note book unravellable,
Mins. incomprehensible,
   Wilting Hon. Sec.

Surveyors insatiable,
Chair. unavailable,
Disaster inevitable,
   Pallid Hon. Sec.
Gardeners querulous,
Rockeries perilous,
Poor Honorarius
   Timid Hon. Sec.

Professor fanatical
Latin botanical
Correction maniacal,
  Frantic Hon. Sec.
Newsletter critical,
Deadline tyrannical,
Printer illogical -
  Panic Hon. Sec.

Letters all readable,
Spelling acceptable,
All are amenable,
  Euphoric Hon Sec.
Luncheon quite edible
Speaker delectable,
Blushes detectable,
  Ecstatic Hon. Sec.

Daphne Lawry

A QUIET HOUR

Take time to stand in your garden
and you will see some wonderful things
A busy bumblebee, the beauty of a
                            butterfly's wings
The unfolding of the first poppy petals
Oh the joy that brings

The glory of a cloudless blue sky
The rays from a warm sun
A new rose just opened, on a new day
                            just begun
With nature surrounding you in your
                    garden, you will be at one

When you take time to stand in your
garden, the problems in life seem far away
in this lovely place, you will find courage,
strength and faith, for the tasks in life
                            every day.

Marion Henderson

SEASON'S BEAUTY

Winter woe on leafless bough
Save for the evergreen
The frost upon the branches show
A tingling glistening sheen
Yes all the season's beauty
Come spring the crocus and daffodil,
And green tips show through the earth
Pleasant even the box on window sill
While in the garden wild birds search
Yes all the seasons beauty
Summer is here in splendid gown
The tree in all its majesty
The garden scents and flowers abound
With harlequins bright jestry
Yes all the seasons beauty
Autumn arrives and flora's change
Tints of red and gold to see
And garden borders we rearrange
For this quarters pleasantry
Yes all the seasons beauty.

H Bradford

GOD'S LITTLE ACRE

A symmetrical square of grass with five conifer trees so forlorn,
We planned and toiled and worked the earth so see our garden born,
We excavated a corner for a quiet place to sit,
Digging down we moved the soil, in a wheelbarrow bit by bit,
We enclosed it with a wall leaving an entrance and an arch,
What a perfect place to sit escaping the winds in March,
With gravel quickly laid and a swinging seat in place,
Herbs in terracotta pots, we found them all a space.

A winding block paved path, a majestic pergola built,
Climbing roses and clematis, I pray that they won't wilt,
Old fashioned plants sown closely leaving no place for a weed,
An abundance of perennials and bedding plants sown from seed,
A raised bed walled by stone, home for a weeping crab apple tree,
Blossom in the springtime, branches falling free,
Clematis cascading down from a neighbours fence,
A rockery with spreading plants forming a carpet dense.

Roses, lupines and foxgloves, far too many to mention,
Rhododendrons, pansies and primroses and a lovely gentian,
Blue-tits nesting in a box upon the chimney breast,
A pair of visiting doves looking eagerly to build their nest,
You do not need to strive for a Sissinghurst or Kew,
With just a tiny plot and patience you can have a garden too,
For a garden is peace on earth a symbol of God's little acre,
With visiting birds and bees all created by our Maker.

Bobby Rashley

CONVERSATION WITH A BLACKBIRD

Come, my friend! I will not harm you!
It takes so little to alarm you!
You've hovered close throughout the year.
You'll need my help now winter's here,
As with your feathered friends you come
To feast upon each scattered crumb.
Although you will accept my crust,
You will not give me all your trust!
You live your wild life in your way
But we meet together every day.
My companion, you have been around
When I've been working on my ground.
With pleasure, I observed your nesting,
Your babies in my hedging resting.

You laboured well to rear your young -
Precariously to life they clung -
But helpless were both you and I
When raiding rooks swept from the sky.
As time went on, I missed your mate -
Did next-door's cat decide her fate?
How fraught with risk your whole life long,
Yet still you trill your rooftop song,
Whilst I, in comfort, fret and frown
When little problems get me down.
I hope you'll in my garden stay.
I'd miss you if you went away.
You watch me with a wary eye -
We respect each other, you and I!

Lynn Gates

DUSK

Stand outside under a summer moon,
And smell a philadelphus bloom.
Honeysuckle, stock and foxglove spire,
Glow now with inner silver fire.

Feel the hush as quiet night falls,
Brushing silky, white roses and all
The silent flowers with drops of moonlight,
Around the velvet darkened pool.

Frenzied daytime insect hum is stilled,
And every plant and flower spike pauses
In its restless growth to breathe out,
Clear, oxygen renewing air.

An owl silently glides through the dusk,
Moths hover and fly quietly
To open evening flowers,
Somewhere a bat barely agitates the dark.

Breathe deeply then, those fragrant stars,
Stand barefoot on fertile earth,
Renew kinship with the trees,
Rooted, firm against the gentle breeze.

For this is the garden's magic hour,
When every bed and every bower,
Is a soothing sanctuary in a maddened world,
And all the petals, pearls.

Sue Chadd

MY GARDEN

Oh, to have a garden like the ones seen on TV,
With sweeping lawns and flowerbeds, a lovely sight to see.
The roses and geraniums around a rustic seat,
The pansies and lobelia make an edging, oh so neat.
A fountain splashing gently like music to the ear,
The goldfish swimming lazily in a pool so cool and clear.
The bluebells and the violets grow in a hidden, woodland glade,
Scented primroses like the stars shine under leafy shade.

Against the overwhelming odds, my garden struggles on,
Slugs and snails and greenfly, my plants, they feed upon.
The clematis and passion flower have climbed a neighbour's tree,
She gets all the flowers and none bloom there for me.
My ponds are full of duckweed, a home for newts, toads, frogs,
The patchy grass is not a lawn, but a stopping place for dogs.
A heron ate the goldfish several years ago,
So now it is just nature and the wildlife show.

But I love my little garden, and I do grow beans and peas,
Strawberries and raspberries, just right for summer teas.
Tomatoes, beets and lettuce, to make a salad lunch.
Mint and sage and parsley, to make a fragrant bunch.
Blackberries and apples, to make delicious jelly.
I really wouldn't want to swap for one seen on the telly!

Jeanne Hollett

LITTLE HANDS

'Shall I put these here grandad?'
Little hands holds up the bulbs
'Aye love, that's right.'
Old hands, sighs and watches
Little hands carefully plants
Next spring's colours
'Next spring up they'll come bright and yellow.'
Old hands rests a while
Leans on his spade, the autumn sun
Warms his aching bones.
Little hands digging, old hands guiding
The circle of seasons continue
Little hands works
Old hands remembers while resting on his spade.

Mary Walsh

NATURE'S RETURN

I have a narrow garden at the back of my terraced house
it's home for cats and birds and at night a fox or mouse
I view it from my kitchen right here in all its glory
the colours of plants and flowers each one has its own story

Sometimes the cat two doors away will silently enter in
and round my legs so gently make sure I know it's him
I'm glad they find a haven, for this is heaven to me
as long as I am able to view the rear fir tree

For firs they speak of endless growth
and every spring from nature's source
I see the snowdrops then the green
of daffodils once hidden now seen

The frost is gone it's time to dig
my birthday present of roses big
there's Cheshire Life and Pascali
they'll bloom when time for summer tea

Around the shed there's passion flower
which yields its fruit o'er many hours
it forms a picture in the front awning
and there I sit to watch nature dawning

At times I'll clear the weeds away
and often in autumn with leaves I'll stay
and gather up all that nature's worn
to find another plant's new-born

No matter how many hours I spend
I'll never repay the garden's trend
of giving life and beauty here
while we grow older year by year.

Lorna May Noah

THE GARDEN IS . . .

                a loathsome thing
On a bitter day when it's not quite spring.
When earth stands hard as iron

And I can't dig up the sod
Where some heavy-footed stranger accidentally trod.
But
In the flash of a ray of sunshine
A blue haze of crocus glows.
As the light lengthens,
Peonies and roses blush
Warming the days even more.
Lilies fill the air with fragrances
Echoed by nicotiana at nightfall.
Butterflies mark the hours
As the buddleia stretches towards autumn
And the burnished fallen leaves of acer
Remind me of winter fires and the buying of seeds.
Full turn the seasons,
Full spins the wheel.
Welcome the heavy-footed stranger
Spring comes at his heel.

Kathryn A Booth

FROM MOTHER NATURE

July arrives and with her brings
A cloud of pretty white and pink
Myriads of bridal blossom
Creamy froth to lace the garden
Tiny bud on fine-stemmed panicle
Fairy drumstick, soft, ephemeral,
Begging birth of dream and myth,
Gysophila or *Baby's Breath*.

Katherine E Philp

THE GARDENERS' RESURRECTION

With arthritic fingers fumbling
And fluid knees a-crumbling
The sound of gardeners grumbling
Is never heard.

Instead their joy is blooming
With nature's growth, assuming
The sun is now consuming
Winter's night.

For through the glasshouse streaming
The rays of warmth are beaming
Melting frost that's gleaming
On the ground.

Like magic, shoots are springing
The bulbs that will be bringing
The blooms, like songbirds singing
Of new birth.

Gardeners never think of dying
But of dormant seeds left lying
And the prospects of defying
Death and decay.

Each spring they set forth sowing
And watch in wonder growing
The rebirth of life, all owing
To God's care.

Ian Boddy

MY GARDEN

My little bit of heaven. My third of acre joy.
The happiness you've brought me nothing can destroy
As a shambles I first saw you, neglected and forlorn,
My heart went out to you at once, my love for you was born.
I felt my hands a-twitching for spade and fork and hoe.
Longing to rearrange you, just couldn't wait for *go*.
Several years have come and gone, my dream has come to pass,
A leafy, scented haven with flower bedecked grass.
Solace from the hectic world where war and strife abound.
The trilling of a passing bird and lazy, buzzing bee, such treasures
                                                          here are found.
In thinking of the early days when heartache was my lot
You clung to me and helped me through my blessed garden plot.
Each day I thank the Lord above for giving me this place.
A joyful and a happy thing, with golden memories laced.

Kathleen Leonard

CHOCOLATE-BOX GARDENS

'This property needs some attention,'
But somehow they didn't quite mention
      the garden was Eden reversed -
All plant-jumble, ant -jungle , cursed.
Wet-wild grass lay strangled with weeds
Paths choking with sycamore seeds,
Fern fronds rusted wrought-iron twisted
Struggling hedges greybeard misted
Cobweb-quilted crumbling deadwood
Care-cold and bleach-blond, the garden stood.

Then I saw, as the sun crept through,
All the flowers in the earth below . . .
I imagined the lawns and the bushes
Deep flower-borders, lily-ponds, rushes

And fat, rounding cabbages, row upon row
The thick chocolate earth, churned to flakes with the hoe
The plant-pots and seedlings, the glasshouse and shed
The birch trees green-silver, the acers' deep red
The snake-twisting hosepipe enticing the scent
      from neatly shaped borders and cyclamen bent
      on the white trellis next to the sun-welcome door
      where slit-eyed, the cat curls asleep on the floor . . .
And all I could see in my dreams the next dawn
Were chocolate-box gardens . . . *laid to lawn.*

Rita Woodall

THE LIVING GARDEN

Beneath the pendulous silver birch
a squirrel sits, on his face a smirk,
holding a nut between his paws,
chosen from the leaves and haws.
A blackbird hops around the urn
searching for a juicy worm,
his wife a browny, paler shade
sits and watches from the glade.
A robin, making up his map
invites a rival to a scrap,
beak to beak they bob and weave,
the newcomer decides to leave
and find a friendlier patch of garden
where pickings might be less hard and
folk might throw out crumbs and seed
to a poor redbreast in time of need.
In the pond newts swim and slither
surrounded by the clumps of heather.
Upon a lily, fat and bulging
sits a frog, blinking and wondering
if he'll ever catch his food,

feeling not really in the mood
for hopping nor a swim,
flies seem scarce, he's getting thin.
With a sort of gallic shrug
he hops beneath an ancient trug.
No use sitting full of sorrow,
always try again tomorrow.

Michael Staniforth

THESE MAKE ME LAUGH

Beneath the shelter of my eaves
Two brown and speckled mallard eggs
Are bedded in the mint that hugs my stable door.
The garden is awash with pale, puce, pregnant poppies.
A shy, green woodpecker briefly pauses on the lawn,
Cocks its head and listens
And here am I, as is my wont,
Washing out the blackbirds' bath water.
- I should be digging.

Dwarf delphiniums now six-feet-nine blue inches high
As thick in girth as a giraffe's neck,
Stand isolated in the border
On stems no gale could snap.
While I am here washing out the blackbirds' bath water
- Instead of digging.

Like a deflated tyre, the grey snake
Flops off the wall to the shade.
He curves and curls his watchful way
To the shadow of the tree and vanishes.

All these and a little, yellow frog
Long legging through the feverfew
These make me laugh
While washing out the blackbirds' bath water.
- Where is the spade?
- I must be digging.

Dorothy Francis

GRANDMA BIRCH'S GARDEN 1934

A child in the garden
Found peppery lupins overhead
It was a jungle of perfume and bees
Of blue sky and glorious colour
It was a damson tree to climb
Chickens, worms and scurrying sun beetle
It was eternity
It is a memory.

Eileen King

THE BIRCH TREE

A slender tree,
Bark silver-white,
Its twigs and branches bare
Until the silent snow
Encrusted them with silver filigree
Etching cold beauty
Against the sombre sky.

Slowly the sun
Dissolved the dull-grey canopy of cloud
And touched the frozen tree
With warmth and light

Melting drop by drop
Its icy covering
Till still more beautiful it shone
In winter's gentle light
Its branches hung with transient diamonds.

Phyllis Moore

THE STRUGGLE

Oh, how I long for winter days
When the spade is laid to rest
For hours, all the summer long
I've toiled to do my best.

The onions, fed, and watered
Succumbed to bolt and rot
Tomatoes dropped their blossoms
And whitefly scourged the lot!

Turnips, swedes and cabbages
All brassicas, I'm told
Got clubroot, scab, and brown heart
The peas went grey with mould.

My limbs grow tired and weary
My boots are caked with mud
Was all that effort worth it
To grow the humble spud?

The flowers too were stricken
With aphids, slugs, and snails
The squirrels ate the crocus bulbs
In spite of nets and nails.

They say hope springs eternal
One day, will I succeed
In killing every garden foe
And strangling every weed?

The answer to the question
Is not in any doubt
I'll never combat nature
Come rain, come shine, come drought.

Audrey Moody

MY BIRTHDAY PRESENT

For my birthday I was given a tree
It was called a Bonsai
But was just a little tree to me
I was told to feed it once a week
So I did what I was told
I also started to speak
And it grew strong, healthy and old
I gave it all my attention
But after a while it started
It went all brown and shrivelled
And that's when we parted
It was taken to the compost heap
Where it could be put to good use
I now make do with a memory
Of my tiny, little spruce.

S Neale-White

GARDEN OF DREAMS

Where summer colours abound
Tumbling tiers of assembled splendour
Perform in ceremonious silence
To herald the welcome we desire

From shady avenues in pastel tones
And fragrant havens with ashen veils
Beside turf best kept for woods to roll
To marvel at such glorious riches

Dancing spangles cascade from rock
Caught in rippling pools of ornate charm
Where secrets are found at the water's edge
Or lost in the fountains of seasons past

Search no more for cherished gifts
That gladden the lives of many who choose
To select their offering without design
And abandon trace of gathering fame

The wayside turns the wheel full circle
Captured moments will again be displayed
In a garden of dreams always remembered
While the steppingstones lead to the rainbow's end.

Keith Bowler

AUTUMN

Silvery cobwebs hang
In foggy silence,
Lacy drapes on the dripping fence.
Their intricate patterns
In delicate thread
Contrast the decaying leaves

In red, gold heaps
On the brown earth beneath.
Their musty smell rising
To speak of the time of year.
In autumn now
Droplets of water
Form on the seed heads,
Decorate old stalks,
And help the natural process
Of returning to earth,
Goodness and nutrients
For regrowth in the spring.

Kate Brown

A GARDEN IN SPRING

In a corner, by a garden shed,
Cowslips bow their dainty head.
Borders along fence and wall, display
Tulips, bluebells and daffodils, so gay.

Spread underneath a lilac tree
In cosy informality,
Hyacinth, pink and white and blue,
Mingle with primula of every hue.

There's iris, crocus and anemone,
With upturned faces for all to see.
Roses in their neatly made bed
Wait for June, mulched and fed.

A greenhouse full to overflow
With bedding plants for a summer show.
Blossom on cherry and plum
Show promise of fruits to come,

Fragrant clusters of vibernum;
And the golden beauty of laburnum;
Verdant grass, unfurled leaves,
A garden in spring, welcome as Achates.

A P Hilton

TREASURED MEMORIES

This garden mine, for thirteen years,
Brings back memories, joy and tears,
Babies, parents, family pets,
I loved it all with no regrets.

So many memories does it hold,
Children playing, tales untold,
Hiding in rhodies, sitting in trees,
Fun games and laughter, grazes on knees,

Spring does come, colours so bold,
Birds all singing in trees so old,
Squirrels so frisky, running around,
Foxes come creeping, not make a sound;

My Dad so frail, loved by us all,
Watches the dragonflies, out by the pool,
Frogs do croak, green woodpeckers laugh,
Butterflies glide up the long, winding path.

Blossom so fragrant, so sweet in the breeze,
Enjoyed by my family, who are so at ease,
Mother still potters in greenhouse and shed,
Growing on seeds to plant out in the bed.

Children are grown now, but when in deep thought,
Remember the garden, their big, wooden fort,
Tricycles, bicycles, trolleys and carts,
Keeps their childhood so strong in their hearts,

All these years have gone so fast,
Holding memories of our treasured past,
My father has gone now, but still he is here,
Held in my garden, so close and so dear.

Rita Seward

BEAUTY ABOUNDS

Four seasons of hard work, performed with love and pride,
A garden of my own, an oasis of my own creation,
My friend when company lacks, a new visitor each day,
A feeling of wealth, my natural treasure trove.

Spring brings expectancy, hope from brave snowdrops,
Summer brings peace, with the warmth fragrance of roses,
Autumn brings fire, and the heat of chrysanthemums,
Winter brings crispness, with jasmine the sun.

Without the love of a garden, a human must lack,
The sense of achievement, the pride of consumed bounty,
A feeling of nature, so strong and so powerful,
That here man is no leader, your garden is king.

Jocelyn Banthorpe

LOVE AFFAIR

Long ago and far away
I saw beautiful nasturtiums
      Growing in a bed
Around a tree, in every shade
      Of yellow, orange, red

Later on, it was my dream
When planning my own garden
      Toiling all the day
With fork and spade, that there, would grow
      nasturtiums, come what may

Seeds and plants, were all put in
Tended with such loving care
      Dealing with each pest
Few seeds came up, plants did not thrive
      Although they'd had the best

Many a try, then I gave up
Growing other lovely flowers
      Blooming, looked so gay
Still I would thrill, to see my love,
      Nasturtiums, when away

Time passed by, another place,
A ready planted garden, but
      Daring, as could be
Nasturtium seeds, I poked them in
      Along the rockery

Now at last, I have my dream,
They're growing, spreading everywhere
      Climbing, just a maze
Of colour bright, from gold to red
      Cheering my autumn days.

Dorothy Dosson

THE FORMAL BED

The annual plants in the formal bed,
Require little attention but to be watered and fed.
They establish, mature and for certain repay,
All the effort put in for them to display.
Tall in the centre red-pink snapdragons grow,
Strong as they tower above all else below.
Around them kochia, as green as the lawn,
Adding interest, even though, no flowers are borne.
And helping to form a symmetrical circle,
Are the showy petunias, with their petals of purple.
Close by calceolarias with their slippers of yellow,
Proving a colourful and worthwhile bed-fellow.
Next to add contrast to the floral display,
Is the ice cineraria dressed in silver-grey.
And the stocks arrayed in pink and white bloom,
Sway in the breeze and release their perfume.
Whilst the salvias with petals of flaming red,
Blaze like a fire in the soil where they spread.
And the tagetes gleam when their buds unfold,
Displaying their shades of yellow and gold.
Amongst them ageratum perhaps not the best,
But they add gentle colour to blend in with the rest.
Around the edges, there's white lobelia too,
Beside them their namesakes but flowering blue.
And with the lobelia to help form the border,
There's the bi-coloured limnanthes keeping low growing order.
With the blue nemophila with its leaf like a feather,
Placed here and there to keep the border together.
Pink, red, purple, blue, yellow, gold and white,
In summer formal bedding is such a delight.

James Walters

SHORT LIVES

    Cold and dark, the surrounding earth
life lies dormant beneath the stark winter skies
warmth from the still weak sun worms through the soil
tepid fingers caress the still, embryonic plant

Tentative tendrils seek a glimmer of light
refreshing rains encourage quicker growth
until at last, the earth shows green
leaves emerging from their winter chrysalis

Upwards and outwards, faster and faster
a race toward the ripening sun
greenery thickening, buds forming
the pinnacle of the year approaching

Plump petal cases unfold in a riot of colour
gentle breezes carry the scents of summer abroad
the still air echoes to the sound of bees
ensuring further propagation of life

Idyllic summer days a fading memory
petals fading, foliage dulling
slowly, with the shortening of the days
life begins to ebb away

When autumn winds sweep across the cooling land
stalks and stems turn to husk
their former glory but a memory
the life sap drains, the plant is gone.

R F Trollope

THE GARDEN CHANGES

You grew me roses, deep, red, red roses,
Wide borders delighted with their colours and form.
Iris, phlox and lupins mixed well with the daisies,
Pink and white blossom promised fruit in the fall.
And I looked around thankful for the pleasure it gave.

But roses grow old, mossy, gnarled and fade,
Rosemary grows where once they did flourish,
Thyme, mint and sages fill the air with perfume
Old apple trees leaning, give shade from the sunshine,
Green grass is mown where fewer flowers are grown.

You left me red roses, now just one remains.
It shines through my sorrow, it helps me remember
The joys of the weeding, the sowing, the plans which we made.
Hope is the life force, the garden the healer.
Today I give you red roses, can roses ever fade?

Muriel Grindley

LOVE'S GARDEN

My love gave me a garden
Where nature ruled sublime
To create order out of chaos
He said, would help to pass the time

My love built me a greenhouse
Wherein fine seeds to sow
To raise and then plant out
He said, would make a lovely show

My love built me a compost box
With strong and seasoned wood
With lessons on with what and how
To make my garden good

My love built me a cold frame
All glazed and hinged and bright
To put my growing seedlings in
He taught me to do it right

My love bought me a mower
With gears and power for speed
And a box to catch the grass in
He said, 'Just what you need.'

My love built me a garden seat
Whereon I might recline
To view the efforts of my work
The creation that was mine

But it is he that on it always sits
In warm spring and summertime
With planting, weeding, pruning, mowing
I never have the time.
Jill Collingham

IN AN ALLOTMENT GARDEN

I sit and dream of summers to come,
    warm moist air and gentle rain.
Caressing the blooms and the soft green leaves.
    Branches sway in a gentle breeze.

I feed the birds to carry them through,
    to nest in the boxes safe and secure.
All kinds of animals feeding together
    battling to survive the worst winter weather.

In the pond the plants have survived.
    In the mud at the bottom a frog sits wide-eyed.
Millions of creatures waiting dormant and still,
    longing for the departure of winter's chill.

In the wild flower patch there's a pile of logs,
    to attract the insects or a stray hedgehog.
A group of stones hides the slugs and snails,
    the warm, spring sun shows their glistening trails.

I've dug in the compost, sorted this year's seed.
    I'll try to be organic with their summer feed.
Little lettuce and cabbage have survived the snow.
    In egg boxes seed potatoes are beginning to grow.

Summer's here at last, but there's still lots to be done.
    I'm already looking ahead at the new year to come.
It's an ongoing thing, you'll always find me there,
    giving the land and wildlife my devotion and care.

Penny Lungley

IN MY DREAM GARDEN

From quaint thatched roof soft doves are cooing,
Slick swallows flit among the eaves,
Sensuous blossoms the bees are wooing,
And the golden sun glints through the leaves
Of the grapevine's shady canopy.

A wanton wisteria over the wall is wending,
Drooping her racemes voluptuously,
Then with dazzling cascade descending
Showers her scented chandeliers seductively
Bewitching all who stray too near.

The fragrance of flowers the air pervades -
Roses, lilies, pinks and thyme,
Wafting through the woodland glades,
Blending with sweet honeysuckle in its climb
Through rampant elder, hawthorn and briar.

The breeze blows over the dawdling stream,
Kingfishers skim beneath the willows,
Hot, stifling noon passes as in a dream.
The sun caresses the backs of minnows
And the mayflies court their ladies fair.

As sultry noon gives way to dewy dusk
More subtle beauties come to light -
Evening primrose, nicotiana give up their musk.
Bats and owls begin their evening flight
To forage until the rosy dawn.

Rhona Anne Pointon

BEHIND THE SPADE

When problems weigh upon my shoulders,
And I'm sad the world's in disarray,
When burdens, sometimes never-ending,
Take their toll from day-to-day,
I find a magic in my garden!
It has amazing, soothing powers.
Although the size is 'postage stamp'
I can potter there for hours.

The mind is focused totally;
Each task becomes a work of art;
Weeding, planting, digging -
Seems to come right from the heart.

Sparrows nervously twitter above
(Waiting for me to disappear!)
But not my friend, the blackbird,
He stays so close - he has no fear.

I'm now intoxicated with fresh air -
Nature's secrets all abound;
Oblivious to passing time;
To the world scurrying round.

Yes, that's the magic in my garden;
Clearing and balancing the mind;
Awakening the soul to simple beauty;
Uniting body and earth; Creator and mankind.

Valerie Jackson

COLOUR CODED

How lovely is a garden
In all its many hues,
The warmth of yellow, orange, red,
The coolness of the blues.

A corner there where pink looks good
A dazzling white just here,
We paint with flowers a picture
To bring us months of cheer.

And then as nature changes
And brings us cooler days,
Autumn takes the palette
And with bronze and yellow plays.

A rest now for the garden
As winter comes to stay,
But even so a colour gleams
In some dark corner, tucked away.

Why is it with the flowers
That in the border grow,
Bold colours blend with ease and grace
to make a special show?

How lovely is a garden
In all its many hues,
A canvas painted just for us
To chase away our blues.

Hazel H Mingham

MY GARDEN SHED

There is an accumulation of gardening tools
In my garden shed
Along with an assortment of nets for the pond
In my garden shed.

There are chairs that I use in the garden,
Canes and plant-pots too
And some string for tying up plants with -
That reminds me, it's a job I must do!

Whenever I can't find a spray or a jar
I look in my garden shed
When I want an odd bit for the car
It'll be in my garden shed.

There are things I remember from my childhood
The old seat from the swing that broke
The head that came off my best boy doll
A wheel from my bike - with no spokes!

It's the sort of place that is homely
There's an old tatty mat on the floor
And old net curtains at the window
That were around during the last war!

It would be a bonus if I ever found an objet d'art
Whilst rooting in my garden shed
Lurking 'neath the spades, forks and old dead flowers
That are in my garden shed.

There's another thing I often wonder
(And I feel it must be said)
'Do you keep such a treasure trove
In your garden shed?'

Monica Brooke

A GARDENER'S DILEMMA

A hosta near that wall I'd grown
Where now the ivy trails.
A perfect meal, had I but known,
For creeper harbouring snails.

The devastation that I found
Deprived my heart of joy.
I'd have to scatter pellets round
Those molluscs to destroy.

But then I heard a knock, knock, knock,
Which made me catch my breath.
That Song thrush shelling snails on rock
Would be their cause of death.

Not so! For while that speckled bird
Ate snails when hours were light,
More of its prey, unseen, unheard
Devoured my plant at night!

Now though it really makes me sad
To kill a garden pest
And glorious birdsong makes me glad,
I love my hosta best.

Yet if those snails are not to thrive
But wither by my hand,
The Song thrush may not long survive
To beautify our land.

Hence my dilemma, as you see
From all I've had to tell.
If I'm a gardener, can I be
A naturalist as well?

Vivienne Tuddenham

UNTITLED

I like to walk around our garden
When the day is very new,
While shadows lie across the flowerbeds
And grass is interlaced with dew.

A garden has so many secrets
Which the seasons will lay bare,
Surprises wait round every corner,
Anticipation draws me there.

An unexpected bulb or seedling,
A lovely flower without a name,
An unknown perfume, sweet and heady -
A garden never stays the same!

Perennials, loved and greatly treasured,
Every spring will reappear.
Annuals briefly stay to charm me,
They will tempt again next year.

So much to do, yet time to linger
Where the trees cast gentle shade,
And share the beauty of the garden
With the robin on my spade.

Joan Letts

IT'S ALL WORTHWHILE

Grass invading the flowerbeds, bindweed creeping ever higher up
                                                       the old stone wall
Dried heads of flowers past their prime, a sad memory of them all
Back aching over heavy spade, gloves and boots caked in soil
Can't stop for a cup of tea, can't see an end to all this toil

Stone wall shimmering in the afternoon sun
Flowerbeds dug all spick and span
Daffodil leaves pushing silently through
Snowdrop and crocus blooming as one
Dreams upon dreams of days to come, dozens of cuttings in pots on
                                                        the sill

Seed orders posted, the plan's laid out
Impatience is rising of that there's no doubt

Summer days are here at last, seeds have risen to meet its rays
Nimble fingers prick out and plant, marvelling at the wonder of
nature's ways
Spring flowers have said their final goodbye, bedding plants lined up
in trays
Can't put the deed off any longer, must plant out for a colourful blaze

No rain, no rain the weathermen cry
Hosepipes forbidden, the ground's so dry
Can after can of tap water poured
Bathwater saved and dishwater stored

The heavens open, the rain pours down, battering roses and flower-
heads alike
When will it stop? We've had enough!
Beds under water, more like a dyke!

Late summer days; warm, balmy nights; garden parties and
barbecues
Deckchairs and loungers, fragrance pervading the breeze
The hard work is worth it for evenings like these.

Angela Morley

LAWN GEMS

Man carpets his home with tufty pile
His garden is carpeted nature's style,
With lawns of grass or sometimes clover
But little else, 'Spread weedkiller over,'
Say gardeners who are so very keen,
To have lawns similar to a bowling green.
But how I pity these soulless types
I would scatter daisies and put all to rights.

Gwen Mason

UP THE GARDEN PATH

Wellies at the ready
Secateurs in hand
The winter's nearly over
And we need to tend the land.

Lawns a-growing greener
As shrubs begin to bud
Never mind the weather
Or the beds a sea of mud.

We need to get a-pruning
For the days are drawing out
To clear away the muddle
As the weeds begin to sprout.

The pleasures from a garden
Can be endless and abiding
And Nature plays a major part
In month by month providing

A little time spent planning
Will save a deal of sweat
And give you hours of pleasure
When days are warm and wet

Catalogues keep coming
Pressing us for order
So get that Gardeners' World out
And brighten up those borders.

M Scofield Jones

THROUGH THE GARDEN GATES

I saw a garden through the great, iron gates,
Wonderful and fair, whereon it seemed the fates
Could not destroy the beauteous plan.
I watched each season come and go in turn,
With snowdrops, pansy, columbine and fern;
Banks of flowers far as eye could scan.

Each woodbine, clematis climbed the walls
And red virginia, vivid in the falls;
Amid the rocks exquisite alpines bloomed
But now all's gone of beauty not a trace
Bricks and mortar cover earth's fair face,
The trees are lost, the peace and wildlife doomed.

G Coleman

THE GREEN LOOK

When God invented gardening clubs
He had a simple plan,
To let folk swap ideas and seeds
For betterment of man.

But like all simple plans we know
There's bound to be a hitch
Should God propose or man dispose?
It hardly matters which.

In everybody's gardening club
Is one we do not need,
Who boasts that his beloved plot
Has not a single weed.

I want to answer, 'Mine's like that!'
No single weed in sight
But randy copulating weeds
Increasing as of right.

They're making such a show of it
The thought is in my head
To banish flowers from my beds
And grow the weeds instead.

Bill Johnson

MI YELLA ROSE BUSH

Ah bought a yella rose bush, it didn't cost a lot,
W'en Ah planted it in t' gaarden it flaired reight ont' dot.
Just one single yella rose, that's awl it did that summer,
But Ah just thowt well it must be a laate cummer.

But nay, t' summer after that it nobbut bore mi three,
Ah wer' feelin' reight upset til a gaardner sed tu mi,
Dusti never tawk tu t' trees, Ah sed, Dooan't bi daft,
Awlreight thee laff tha'll find, 'e sed growin' stuffs a craft.

Ah luket at t' bush an' wundered cud thowd mon bi reight,
Eny rooad Ah'll try it w'en Ah've 'ad summat tu eit,
W'en Ah've 'ad mi tae Ah thowt Ah'll try thowd gaardner 'int.
Ah didn't waant tu loise it tho it 'adn't cost a mint.

Ah thowt at furst cajole it, then Ah thowt Nay will Ah 'eck,
It's time it shappet it dozey sel' i' muck up tu it neck.
So Ah stood theer an' Ah shaiuted, just lissen 'ere thee,
Ah'll gi'e thi til next summer tu prove thisel tu me.

Ah'll sweer Ah see it tremble as Ah finished mi tirade,
But Ah thowt enuff's enuff neaw, it can aither bloom er fade.
Well t' truth is this summer that rose bush wer' a treet,
Yella roses i' profushon wer' ev'ry weer in t' seet.

Esma Banham

BEING NEIGHBOURLY

I've done my good deed for today,
For you folks who live over the way.
The flowers in the tubs
The peach tree and such,
I've watered while you've been away.

Through the cherry is losing its fruit,
The garden is looking real cute.
The sweet peas are in flower
And the lovely rose bower
Is hanging with bloom, a real beaut.

There's a rose in a pot, really sweet,
I've gazed at each day, quite a treat.
Osteospermums galore.
Round by the door,
The likes of which cannot be beat!

The clematis in the greenhouse,
Was admired by myself and my spouse,
Grapes by the score,
As you walk in the door
You've to duck, lest the peach knock you out.

And soon you will make your way home,
You'll be glad when your journey is done.
And as you unpack,
Say 'It's nice to be back,'
And the garden will say 'Welcome home.'

Olive Smith

UNTITLED

Born of a family from the land.
Quite in contrast to walking the strand.
Gardening over the years is all I've really known.
Very rewarding it has been I'm sure I'm not alone.
As a youngster the keenness was there
Learning the basics needed great care.
Not very exciting was the washing of pots.
Then soon after came the weeding of plots.
Later the art of pruning was sought,
Not too long or not too short.
The Latin names were quite a task.
If you didn't know you had to ask,
As time advanced I had use of a spade,
Then it was not long before seed bed was made.
Straight lines of seedlings soon appeared,
Resembling the growth of a veterans beard.
The time soon came to do some thinning
I knew then that I was actually winning,
Came the harvest with its tasty fresh produce
All of which was put to very good use,
During the war the response was outstanding
'Growmore' was the cry, readily expanding
The demand for fertiliser was never greater.
In producing early crops rather than later
Now that organics have appeared on the scene,

There's no need to tell you everything is green.
Retirement is here, so I have one request
To be able to cope just like the rest.

P T Dover

MY GARDEN

I wish I had a garden
where herbs and flowers grow,
with sweetly scented lavender
and roses in a row.

I'd find a little sunny spot
where I would take my chair,
and I would sit and ruminate
and sniff the scented air.

But my True Love breeds chickens -
oh! how they scratch and cluck -
and where there should be pansies
there is feathers, holes and muck.

The ducks come off the river
to eat up all the slugs.
They also pick my flowers
to fill their hungry mugs.

And if by chance
should some green sprouts
come up to greet the sun,
the pigmy goat leaps over the wall
and nibbles every one.

Oh! I wish I had a garden!
The best thing I can do
is to cover the lot with concrete
and call it a Children's Zoo.

Sheila Holligon

A GARDENER'S DREAM

Please Mr Slug, eat my weeds,
I unwillingly provide all your needs.
Dandelion, dock, the list has no end,
So, please Mr Slug, start a new trend.
Tell all the family to let my veg be
Chick weed or nettle, eat them, feel free.
Pass the word to your friends, the eelworm and snail.
If they keep the bargain, my garden won't fail.
I promise no pellets or beer traps,
Just keep off the lettuce, there's good chaps.
One section of plot, I will leave to provide,
Nooks and crannies, all places to hide,
From birds and hot sun, on warm summer days,
So, please Mr Slug please mend your ways.

D M Lee

RAIN

Listen to the rhythm of the falling rain
Natures lifeblood on the world again
Glistening pearl drops, April showers
Bringing forth the springtime flowers.

Misty morning soaked with dew
Pristine freshness to a dawn that's new
Streams that twist like a country lane
Listen to the rhythm of the falling rain.

Moody rivers babbling brooks
Peaceful lakes with mirrored looks
Winters grip has lost again
Listen to the rhythm of the falling rain.

K Sutton

A WILDLIFE GARDEN

My garden is a wilderness,
But not untidy, I might stress,
There's trees and shrubs and native flowers,
Where squirrels play for hours and hours.
There's sparrows, blue tits, magpies too,
There's yellow cowslips, and bells of blue,
There's primroses and oxlips rare
And a natural pond with lilies where
Frogs and newts may swim and breed,
So their offspring will succeed
In giving pleasure to those who might
Follow me and continue the fight
To save our wildlife and native flowers,
From the dark and terrible powers,
That seem intent on destroying all,
Causing the whole of our planet to fall
Into total disrepair -
Tell me, do you think that's fair?
Then join me - don't just sit and moan -
Create a wilderness of your own!

Pete Perry

HOW MANY TIMES

How many times has she been seen,
Clearing her garden of weeded green,
She tends her garden with loving care,
She still has beauty, bright and fair.

She has very many friends,
and her hospitality, she extends,
She's never bored or lonely,
As she explains, she's far too busy.

In her garden are many more friends,
Crocus, Narcissus and daffodils,
All sorts of herbs for curing ills,
She doesn't believe in chemists pills.

She cultures every plant with honour,
She waters them and sees them flower,
Crocus, narcissus, she loves them all,
But loves her daffodils most of all.

How many times has she been seen,
Clearing her garden of weeded green,
She tends her garden with loving care,
She still has beauty, bright and fair.

Leslie William Bullock

MY NEIGHBOUR'S CHERRY TREE

It's coming out, it's coming out, it's only early May,
We noticed it, we noticed it, we looked at it today,
It stands so tall and stately at the edge of lawn
Get up, get up and look at it, at very early dawn.

Its petals are so pretty, so pretty pink and pearl,
The leaves are very pretty too, now they've started to uncurl.
You thought that it had been attacked by every common bird
They must have heard your grumbling,
They listened and they heard.
Your visitors will admire it,
When they come to tea,
As they walk right up the path,
They'll see your lovely Cherry Tree.

Mollie Bramble

A SEED

It looked so small and lifeless
As I held it in my hand
So tiny, and so helpless
Just like a grain of sand.

And yet, within that minute speck
Lay, hidden from my eyes
A marvel of the universe
Of pleasure, and surprise.

Its needs were simply stated
Moisture, soil and light
And then a little extra warmth
To waken it from night.

So, just a few days later
Some leaves began to show
And, with a little tender care
Continued so to grow.

I placed it in the border
To feel the sun and rain
And watched it grow and prosper
Full stature to attain.

The flower buds formed then opened
Oh! What a lovely sight
The colour and the perfume
Still fills me with delight.

To call this tiny thing a seed
Must be to understate,
The secret life that's hidden in
A miracle so great.

Horace Hartley

DREAM GARDEN

Amazing borders full of enchanting promise
Restful vistas, uncompromising splendour
Our dreams of gardening ambitions realised
Missed opportunities alas we sit and ponder
The seasons depart the shadows lengthen
Dappled hues reassuring reflective waters
Hopes, thoughts and loves nature's wonder
Glorious summer worthwhile treasured moments
The heritage remaining a sight of heaven
Blooms so vibrant the trials of nature
Everlasting glories, bright transient memories
The years pass quickly so emphatically
If only we had given more of lazy days spent
Your small domain in tatters so dramatically
A few more hours of effort beset with intent
The Judas tree not full of woe is heaven sent
Camellias, carmine and pink, florid displays so elegant

Ivy, roses, clematis, clambering, clinging to compete
Distant bells, melodic and soulful from lofty spire
Hopes shattered by will, a practical defeat
The task is complete but only if you pardon
It looks remarkably fine, if only self deceit
So please imagine, imagine if you will
The inspiration to build your very own dream garden.

Brian William Smith

THE GARDEN PARADE

Dactura blew their trumpets
The parade's about to start
With their feathered plumage head - dress
Comes the elegant pampas grass.

With a jingle come the bluebells
Ringing a merry sound
And fuchsia ballerina's
Are dancing all around.

Behind them come the fern
Waving to the crowd
With beautiful chrysanthemums
Their heads held in the clouds

Along come the dear petunias
Happy as the day is long
Gladiolus fast behind them
Tall and stout and strong.

While sunflowers shine upon them
Spider flowers weave their way
In and out and through they roam
Around the slendour gypsophila.

Here comes the sweet carnations
With relatives doris pinks
And from the crowd that's watching
Black - eyed susan gives a wink.

The parade is at an end now
Lobelia trails up the rear
And going past the willow
It drops a mighty tear.

Sarah Doyle

GARDENERS' WORLD

My garden is a pleasant place
In spring when daffs and crocus race
To greet the lemon sorbet sun
Until east winds flatten them one by one!

My garden is a stunning place
In summer when bright eyed pansies chase
Ivy, ribes and potted ferns
Before losing out to slugs and birds!

My garden is a peaceful place
In autumn when crisp leaves gain space
And cover every bulb and bud
Until rain rots blanket in squelchy mud!

My garden is a special place
In winter when Jack Frost's fingers trace
Patterns on each blade of grass
Before boredom makes him freeze my taps!

Betty Lightfoot

A GARDENERS LAMENT

A garden is a lovesome thing
Or so the poets say.
It's not so very lovesome
When the slugs come out to play.
You plant out tender seedlings
They vanish without trace.
But my Hostas are unusual
Their leaves look just like lace.
There's greenfly on the roses,
The clematis has wilt.
The earwigs eat my Dahlias
And the trellis has a tilt.
I struggle on as gardeners do,
Forever optimistic
But I think that Mother Nature
Can be a bit sadistic
As an interesting hobby
You really cannot whack it.
But I wonder why, when my seeds come up
They don't look like the packet.

M A Read

OCTOBER GARDEN

I greet each new October
With sadness in my heart
For I must clear the borders,
And I am loathe to start,
To know that Summer's over,
That autumn frosts will nip,
And that the cold of winter
Will have earth it its grip.

But the wheelbarrow is ready
And soon it's overfilled
With leaves and weeds and prunings
And petals that have spilled,
And the ground looks dark and wonderful,
The robin sings with glee
As I start turning clods of earth
And set the insects free.

And the sun is very pleasant,
Warming to my back,
And a throaty starling, bold as brass
Calls from on the chimney stack,
And on the bonfire, burning bright
Goes all that's left of the delight
The year has brought.
Now there's no sorrow in the thought,
But gladness
For the earth is bare and free, and so
There's lots of space for next year's
plants to grow.

Dorothy Morris

THE FUCHSIA

The fuchsia dances on her toes,
   Where she finds her beauty no one knows.
She pirouettes round and round
   In her pot or in the ground.

Her tutu pink is flowing,
   Her roots below are growing,
She reaches up towards the light,
   She really is a lovely sight.

The autumn days are drawing in
   Now the colder days begin.
Her leaves fall off, she'll disappear,
   That is until in June next year.

Sarah Louise Appleyard

A LOVELY PLACE TO BE

To me,
My garden is a lovely place to be.
I like to get down on my knees,
And pull the weeds;
And then, to hoe and rake the rows -
To sow new seeds,
And happily anticipate
The burst of new life as they germinate.

I wield
My hand fork and my trowel, and see revealed
The teeming life within the soil.
I irrigate,
I deadhead flowers, and mulch, and prune,
And contemplate
The source of life creating power
Expressed in plants and creatures hour by hour.

I know,
That while my garden's blanketed with snow,
Soil-life abounds not far below -
Safe from the freeze -
Until the springtime surge of growth.
Then, on my knees,
I'll pull weeds for the compost heap,
Rejoicing as my garden wakes from sleep.

I see
A myriad blossoms on the apple tree.
New fruit and vegetables grow;
While herbs and flowers,
Attracting butterflies and bees
Give many hours
Of sweet content . . . and so, for me,
My garden is a lovely place to be.
Jean McDonald

GARDEN FOR ALL SEASONS

There is a gentleness in springtime flowers,
Swaying and bowing in the April air;
Daffodils drifting through the grass in showers,
Crocus and primrose jewel where earth was bare.

There is a glory in the summer's blooms;
Roses, carnations, glow and scent the breeze,
Colourful carpets wov'n by nature's looms,
Blossom on bushes, creepers, shrubs and trees.

There is a richness in the autumn shades;
An ageing beauty, born of life complete;
Fullness of fruit, rich reds and golden glades,
Living fulfilled gives way to life's retreat.

Then winter, dark brown earth and naked trees
Sparkling with frost, or clothed in drifts of snow,
Puddled by rain and mud or stiff from freeze,
Is nature dead? No, resting . . . set to grow!

Gardens are gracious with each season's birth;
Their loveliness abides when our life's done.
May I when time says 'Bid farewell to earth.'
Be seated on our lawn at setting sun!

Olwen France

ANTICIPATION

The daylight hours are shorter,
The sun hides, who knows where
Rain and sleet, have got us beat,
And gardens lie all bare.

But do we feel discouraged?
No, we are a race apart,
Each day brings near, the days that's dear,
To every gardeners heart.

That first bright day of spring,
Warm days that banish rain
So we can wait, anticipate,
The sun will shine again.

Anne Aitchison

UNTITLED

I thank the Lord for my health and strength
I thank him for my garden
It's not as neat as it used to be
For which I beg his pardon
But I'm seventy-three and I do my best
To grow some veg and flowers
And I thank the Lord that I am
Blessed with many happy hours.

P Sears

UNTITLED

Harsh winter cries in voices loud
Through oak and ash, stark and proud,
That heps are but a rose's shroud,
Embalmed by snow from scudding cloud.

Gugnunc

THE CHEAT

Old Culpepper Brown is the talk of the town
He lives along side the old grange
He never says much just shouts at the kids
But the locals all think him quite strange.

When he is happy he whistles a song
Whilst showing his carrot at least a foot long
His marrows are huge, his onions so round
The vicar, just stared and the judges they frowned.

The local Lord Mayor came along to the show
He had heard of Culpepper and the veg he could grow
The Mayor is a gardener of considerable bent
But he had quite a shock when he entered the tent.

A little old lady who came along to the stand
Said to Culpepper this really is grand
Can I have a look at your extra large cauli
And she gave it a poke with the end of her brolly.

It rolled off the stand down onto the grass
Caught the eye of a judge who happened to pass
Picking it up to place on the stand
He noticed a price tag stuck to his hand.

The judge he just stared disbelief on his face
He'd discovered a cheat in this all hallowed place
Culpeppers face was frozen like ice
He'd forgotten to take off the sixty pence price.

He is banished for life from all of the shows
The memories are with him where ever he goes
He's haunted by caulis in dreams not so nice
All of them wearing that sixty pence price.

D Burns

COMPROMISE

The weeds grew crazily in my garden,
The grass erupted like Krakatoa
And everywhere the lilac's urchin children
Pushed with rough vigour through the coarse soil.

Now the lawn at least is neat and tamed,
The roses powdered and shampooed -
Sophisticated beauties - and the ranks
Of marigolds and soldierly geraniums
Give a sense of order to the plot.
But near the roses lurks a gypsy foxglove
I did not plant, the borders swarm with flowers
I cannot name. Or weeds? I am not sure.
The bold bamboo elbows along the fence
And overall the giant princess birch tree
Scatters an unruly dappled shade.

This is a battle I am glad not to win.

John Clifford

MY GARDEN

I have a garden,
There, beyond that wall,
With bergamot and rosemary,
And delphiniums tall.

I love to spend my days there,
Devoting hours and hours,
To tending and caring for
My bushes, trees and flowers.

I have a favourite spot there,
Beneath the greengage tree,
Where sun shines, dappled through the leaves
And bluebells grow wild and free.

In springtime, the robins
Make the potting shed their home,
In summer an empty nest,
The babies, they have flown.

Yes, I have a garden
And hope I always shall,
Be able to spend my days there,
There, beyond that wall.

Christine Morris

STRAWBERRIES

We planted strawberries yesterday.
It was a cloudless day in autumn
When air is soft as April
And the cool soil breaks cleanly.

I sorted plants, setting aside
Those with the largest crowns
And vigorous roots;
You spread old muck, all crumbly
Like shredded pipe tobacco
And set the lines, three spans wide;
Then all was ready.

Each plant was gentled into its place
Roots teased with the fingers
Crowns just proud of the soil
And earth knuckled round them firmly.

At the end of the plot we stood,
Straightened our backs and looked.
Already you were biting
Into the first fruit of next year.
While sharp in my nostrils rose
The aroma of home-made strawberry jam!

Barbara Ellis

THE PASSION FOR GARDENING

The passion for gardening cannot be explained,
It's irrational, perverse and obscure.
What else would make a sane person exclaim -
'I could do with a load of manure?'

There's no sense nor reason in staying up late
When the rest of the world's gone to bed,
With a flash light to hunt down a big slimy slug
In order to chop off its head.

Who else would rush out on a cold winter's night
To cover up plants from the cold,
Armed with fleece, straw and hessian, string and the like,
Or even a curtain that's old -

To ensure that a plant will be cosy and warm,
Protected from frost, wind and ice?
Well, it must be a gardener, mad in the head,
To do this without thinking twice.

The passion for gardening cannot be explained,
It's illogical, wayward and strange,
For people who otherwise seem to be sane
Act almost as if they're deranged.

S M Bell

FERNS

Shady in some hollow grows
Forgotten symmetry of delicate hues
That from before the first petal shone
In the time that only earth knows
As an ecclesiastical staff of office
First shoots arose
And in strength of hooded green
The first sign of new life shows
No flower bright do you carry
Your spore, dust that upon a breath would tarry
No willing slaves do you required
Either in their endless work or bright attire
Only rain that soft caress you desire
To grow arching, across time itself
Yet in such variety to give shadows wealth
When in autumn brown and tan

Spider silver with jewels of dew
Decorate such delicate symmetry as you
Forgotten almost as time
Your arcane beauty into hearts and minds entwine.

Jon Finney

PESTS

Name any species of garden pest
I've got them all, let me tell you the rest,
Slugs and snails and red spider mite
These are a few that I did not invite
Blackfly, greenfly, whitefly too
Have you got these, do they bother you?
If I had a penny for every earwig found,
I'd be so rich, I'd have a million pound.
But all these pests won't deter me a jot
From the garden I love, my peaceful plot.

Andrew Readman

MORE THAN A HOBBY

My garden is not just a hobby,
It's more a part of my life
But keeping it tidy and blooming
Is not without trouble and strife.

My daughter helps me with ever sprouting weeds,
She pulls one and asks 'is this bad?'
Holding one of my new growing seeds
Dangling, wilting and sad.

With such pleasure glowing from her upturned face
I can't bring myself to be cross,
So I show her the bad ones and tell her 'good girl'
And write off my seedlings as loss.

I've got the rockery sorted
The lawn has yet to be sown.
Oh how I long for the day to come
When I can say 'the lawn needs mown!'
Somewhere for David and Emma-Jane
To run and jump and fall -
With bruising, bumps or cuts and scrapes
The garden provides it all.

It's also somewhere for me to hide
To give myself time on my own
I can sit and relax on the rockery seat
And enjoy how my garden has grown.

My garden is not just a hobby
It's more a part of my life
But caring for it with my family
Is worth any trouble and strife.

Louise Corbett

BEHIND THE SPADE

Lightning flashed and thunder battered,
Winds screamed and widely scattered,
When out of the blue
The sun broke through.
Primroses yellow and crocus blue,
Brought joy to all days
In thousands of ways.

Let the rain tumble
We no longer trouble
Wrens and robins chirp and bubble,
Spring is on the way
Is just what they say.

Gone is the gloom
No more is there room
For howling and splatter,
As hedgerows grow fatter.

Lilacs and willows
Put on a display
That's all one can say -
Is surely it's May.

Barbara Voss

IF IT WASN'T FOR THE 'PILLARS IN MY GARDEN

If it wasn't for the 'pillars in my garden
The gooseberry leaves would be all neat and green,
But they eat so carefully round the very edges
That it's easy to espy where they have been.

If it wasn't for the aphids in my garden
The roses would be blooming big and bright,
But they suck right through the bud to sap and juices
And never leave off breeding day or night.

If it wasn't for the snails in my garden
The lettuces would be quite nice to eat,
But they chomp and slurp their way across the middles
And leave those slimy traces with their feet.

If it wasn't for the birdies in my garden
The pears upon the tree would swell and glisten,
But they stab and peck and gouge the fruit all over;
You can hear the little vandals if you listen.

If it wasn't for the nature in my garden
The balance of the world would all be wrong,
They can eat their share of all my garden produce,
I appreciate the happy little throng.

V V Stauber

GROWING WILD

The garden is empty now.
Here and there an unusual, exotic plant preens incongruously in the undergrowth.
A jasmine blooms, a tree's bough bends to kiss a buried stone urn.

Where is the paradise an army of gardeners once fought to keep under control?
Working to create a vision of beauty that their lady inflicted on her surroundings.
All gone.

Reverted to nature.
Hours of toil, planning, waiting for the correct season, cultivating the soil. All in vain.
Vain hope, to tame what is not ours.

The lady now lies silently 'neath a weeping willow.
All activity spent.
The spring breeze brushes lightly through the long grass, but stirs her not to plant fresh seedlings or water young saps.

There is no lasting mark on the earth that she loved so well.
'Cept a moss covered grave where forget-me-nots grow wild.

Kim Hopkinson

SIMPLY NATURE

What a magical place the garden, alive in so many ways,
Whatever the month or the season, on winter or summer days.

The birds come to visit in their hundreds and feed on
                                       provisions therein.
The starlings are the pioneers then the sparrows, thrushes
                                             and wren.

On skilled wing they circle and reconnoitre before coming down
                                             for the kill.
And when they are sure all is safe, they land, for their beaks to fill.

Alas their manners are wanting, for survival makes them
                                             share not.
Whatever food they glean from the garden, they do all to keep
                                             their lot.
The insects and grubs are too busy hunting their food in all its array,
Until it's too late for them to realise they *also* are the food for today.

The birds swoop down and abduct them as their lives they
                                       need to sustain,
And the writhing grub is captured and is part of life's food chain.

The flowers sway silently in the idyllic summer breeze,
Inviting seduction in their clandestine plan with the bees.

Their features are so varied and many; petal, foliage and hue,
For reasons known only to nature - a mystery to me and to you.

We don't *have* to know all of life's secrets, it's here for all to enjoy,
We should accept it for the gift it is, not change it and often destroy!

Nature is manifold and complicated, yet simple, and all are in
                                              the balance,
And if we insist on changing natures ways, it's a terrible game
                                              of chance.
It's a game we cannot possibly win because nature *is* the
                                              strength and might,
She cannot be interfered with and she will always show us
                                              who's right.

So, tarry a while in the garden, breathe in summer scents as
                                              they blow,
Let old mother nature give you her all, and you will see -
                                              it's a fabulous show!

Alan J Cocks

MEALTIME

Dig, dig, earth turned,
Spade in, spade out,
Worm move away,
If you want to live another day,
Bird watching,
Bird waiting,
For a tasty morsel he will choose,
Some he will win,
Some he will lose.
Dig, dig, earth turned,
Spade in,
Spade out,
Watching,
Waiting.

Patricia Gray

SPRING TIME

The garden in spring
Comes alive once again
After the winter
The snow and the rain.

The snowdrop is first,
A primrose is out,
I wonder what next
I'll see spreading about.

Clematis are climbing
The ivy's so tall,
Looks as if both
Are racing the wall.

I'm glad it's so pretty,
The colour and smell
Makes me feel great,
So good and so well.

T B Rees

THE ALLOTMENTS

At night a fox barks, a yapping sound.
I lie in bed listening, it makes my heart pound.
A full moon is shining making it seem eerie.
I try to get to sleep, feeling quite weary.

Whilst in the kitchen, making a bedtime drink.
Staring out at the allotment, standing at the sink.
A bushy tailed fox passes, we both get a surprise.
For a while we just stare at each other, eye to eye.

Long summer days are my favourite viewing.
To watch gardeners busy digging and hoeing.
Tending their well kept rows of veg.
Each separate allotment bordered by fence or hedge.

Where the yellow or white butterflies flutter about.
There a fellow gardener to another, a greeting, will shout.
Occasionally a little field mouse for food will forage.
But beware little mouse, for a cat on the rampage!

Through their own allotment 'jungle' cats like to roam.
Sometimes in on a rodent or bird they will home.
But seagulls swoop down over them with a shrill cry;
For they have chicks in their nests on the roof tops nearby.

Now autumn is over, the harvest been gathered.
Gone is the busy summer that I have favoured.
When the allotments teem with colour, excitement and life.
Now deserted they lie bare, to a long winter's strife.

Sue White

NO LARGER THAN A POSTAGE STAMP

No larger than a postage stamp,
That's what someone said.
A patch of green, a rose or two,
Here and there a flower bed.

Two tomatoes in a gro-bag,
A dozen runner beans I think,
A bird bath in the middle
Where starlings splash and drink.

Daffodils in springtime,
Lovely season of the year,
Hear the blackbird singing
In a voice so loud and clear.

Summer, time for roses,
Daisies tall and white,
Lupins, pretty pansies,
Marigolds orange bright.

All the pretty colours,
All the shades of green,
Bird table, gnomes and other things
To decorate the scene.

Flowers, birds and butterflies,
Ladybird and bee.
My garden, just a postage stamp
But big enough for me.

Patricia Catling

GARDEN GIFTS

Pure blue of sky and linum,
True green of grass and tree,
Deep richness of the roses,
In my garden I can see.
The ivy wanders onwards,
It's shoots a living force,
A clematis brings glory,
As it surges on its course,
The romance of an arbour,
As I sit beneath it's eaves,
The perfume of it's flowers,
The swags of fresh new leaves.

Sweet climbers soften edges,
Bring colour to their host,
Also beauty, blending perfect,
They give to us their most.
The berries ripe and fruitful,
They weigh down bough and twig,
The hips and haws of roses,
Even too the sweetest fig.
I find the bark appealing
It's forms and different hue,
It adds to garden treasures,
And the pleasure it brings to you.
From bird to bee and insect,
Each one will play a part,
In my beloved garden,
Held deep within my heart.

Deidre Ann Bates

THE HERB GARDEN

The herb garden sleeps in the heat of the day,
and over its worn brick paths.
The Thymes and the Marjoram tumble about,
causing the Sages to laugh.

Sweet heady perfume fills the air,
and where the Rosemary grows.
The Tansy stands so straight and tall,
His bright yellow buttons aglow.

By the green Mint and Parsley curls,
a butterfly settles to rest.
It hovers and dithers to make up its mind
which fragrance it thinks is the best.

The Herb Garden gives pleasure to all.
Be it Human and Butterflies wild,
And my sister whose care attends to them all.
Has created a sweet perfumed child.

Ruth M Hart

NOW BEHIND THE SPADE

The sun does shine from day to day
Out in the open without delay
Grab the spade from back of shed
Mark the starting point instead.

Sort out compost, manure heap
Spread it evenly nice and neat
Double dig with spade so grand
The shiniest instrument in the land.

Balanced handle firm and fast
Stainless steel is made to last
Rhythm slow as steady goes
Solid boots protects the toes.

Bend in back makes work easy
High and low, don't get wheezy
A steady stroke to turn the sod
Beats the carrying of a hod.

Constant action gives one thirst
Tea or beer, which comes first
Sit on tub or bench by tree
Have a rest for all to see.

Revitalised, head in skies
Back to digging, is that wise
Make it not too much for sure
Leave some for later, evermore.

The sun is low, it's time for rest
Get the worry off your chest
Great satisfaction is then found
With well dug plot of turned up ground.

Eddie Shaw

BEHIND THE SPADE

Slugs! how they abound
all over the ground
in our English country garden.

Aphids! multiply
as do the greenfly
in our English country garden.

White fly, black fly
down below, up high
black spot, root rot
We've got the lot . . .

It's all such a bore
but we still go on for more
in our English country garden.

Cyril Harding

GARDEN THUGGERY

Oh, what joy it is.
Oh, what bliss!
I've found a kind donor
And it's no misnomer,
Who is willing to support my addiction.
There's always something to suit my predilection;
Marigolds by the score
And delphiniums galore,
Lobelia Cardinalis, tall and scary,
A chomping feat for the wary,
Pansies Universal, mauve and yellow
Have a taste both pleasing and mellow . . .
I'm proud to say I've stripped them bare
Leaving spindly stalks distorted in the air.
I've crawled into containers with summer bedding
And was only discovered in the course of deadheading
I love it where it's dark and damp
And you'll only catch me at night if you use a lamp.
Nowhere is safe from me because I'm a thug.
Yes, you've guessed it I'm a slug!

M Hutchings

LEANING ON A SPADE

Observe the hunting bird
Hang high above his prey
Then drop, taut, taloned to the ground,
And watch as death without a sound
Descends on vole, mole, squirrel, or the fractious shrew.
Should I feel so exalted by its grace
And watch it swing off to some secret place
With pleasure? Should I, say,

Have winced? Even preferred
To see him fail? To feel
The velvet coated vole,
To catch the squirrel's sharp cocked eye
Locked tight on mine, or gently try
To still the quiver of the shrew? I wish I knew.
Perhaps I'll know when earth heaped on my grass
Makes me enquire if I should let him pass
Or cut the beastly mole
In two with this blade's steel!

Patrick Taylor

THE CONSERVATIONIST

Folks tutted at her garden - declared it a disgrace
such weeds all running rampant and wild about the place!
Then came a conservationist - in raptures at the sight
who purred congratulations in paroxysms of delight.

He said 'your Tagets Minuta are really very fine
and this Senico Vulgarise is superior to mine.
I'm bowled over by your Cluckwort (it has an ancient reputation
For soothing upset stomachs and relieving constipation).'

I've never seen such twitch grass - it's invaluable for gout
I wonder - could I have a root when it's time to thin it out?
Your Potentillar Anserina is extraordinarily profuse
(to clear the sin of pimples you just need to drink the juice).

Exploring even further he gasped in disbelief
for growing in the middle was a strange and alien leaf . . .
He scrutinised it eagerly - examining it well
dismayed to find no glorious weed but a Canterbury bell.

(Get a spade and dig it out - he agitatedly insisted
but for that intruder - you could have your garden listed!)

M Boreham

THE LAST ROSE OF SUMMER

The garden lies bleak in the winter gloom,
Standing alone is the last of the summer bloom.
Covered by the fresh sparkling morning dew,
as the sunrise slowly begins the morn anew.
The night's dark cold shadows melt gradually away,
with the warming sunlight of the new day.
It softly crosses the watery petaled bloom shining clear,
The sunlit sparkling scented dew runs, falls as if a tear,
The bloom stands as a reminder of the summer now gone,
the bloom's petals slowly start to fall one by one.
They fall delicately to the waiting ground,
The bloom's petals are spread slowly around.
Like a floral carpet around the bush they lay,
Till wind blows the memories of the beauty away.
The last rose of summer loveliness is now sadly gone,
The flowerless garden now the barrenness is as one.

John Cotterill

UNTITLED

On Saturdays my husband bowls,
my garden I attend.
When digging, weeding, pruning's done
my weary way I wend
up to my cushioned garden seat
with gin, tonic and lemon.
And there I sit, smug and content.
Just viewing my penstemon.

Alice Coles

A GARDEN KNOWS

My favourite paradise
greets me daily,
and summons me forth
about its dimensions.
No ruler sliced borders
nor hedging perfection,
still, my paradise
is my sanctity.

Seasons circumvent
harsh gales subside,
my garden beckons
and I must obey.
Weeks flash by
and blossoms begin,
back breaking labour
rewards, in abundance.

Lush spring and summer
burnished autumn,
will find me there
amongst private heaven.
No words can convey
Emotions I hold,
yet a garden knows
It's gardener's love.

Lynne Tice

THE GARDENER

As evening skies thread skeins of peach against the blue,
and the setting sun dips thankfully to rest,
beyond the greenhouse roof.
An aching back is slowly raised, to once more stand erect.

The toil is over for today, and now amidst sweet scented
flowers and glowing hue,
The gardener breathes the honey scented air,
Content to stand, content to ponder through.
The joys, the pleasures that around him grow.
His old briar pipe is lit with care
and as the first smoke drifts upon the evening air,
he smiles,
and all is well within his heart and view.

Cynthia Byrnes

A DEATH IN THE GARDEN

Where are the others?
Why did I stray so far?
Separated and feeling worried
Lost and not knowing enough
Something is about to happen!

Where are the others?
Why did I not heed their warning?
Everything is tense
Darkness without night
I am trembling with fear!

Where are the others?
Why was I so stupid?
Something huge is falling!
The earth shakes with the crash
It explodes and I am showered by bits!

Where are the others?
Why did they not explain?
Another one is coming and another!
The earth vibrates with the shocks
Shattering, battering, splattering explosions!

Where are the others?
I am trying to run!
But the world is full of flying pieces
I am trapped! I am floundering!
Each one of my six legs are caught!

Where are the others?
What is this terrible thing they called *rain?*
Where . . . aaaaah!

Jenny Owen

A SPECIAL THANK YOU

Our honeymoon has lasted twenty five years
We've shared the worries, sorrows, tears.
Precious memories I recall . . .
And your dear face shining through them all.

Remember our very first home? I do,
It seemed to be made for just me and you
Until that wonderful mid June morn
When our tiny baby son was born.
Then our twosome became three
But still, we were one - you and me.

Remember the little red motorcar?
How we laughed as it took us far . . .
The flowers that you always bought
Even when you shouldn't ought!
Oh! How little we two sought
And what rewards our love has brought.

Days and weeks of constant spring
Even now, can my heart sing
As tender memories I recall . . .
And your dear love, the most of all.

Thelma Watson

THE SPIRIT OF THE GARDEN

The cold, grey blanket of winter is tightly wrapped around today.
Only heath and heather glow punctuates the gloom.
Even knowing of the transience it is still
So hard to believe
That this melancholy scene will explode with new vitality soon.
Yet, less of this hastiness!
This dank bitterness for my eyes is also laughter to my ears.
Laughter from the distant children.
Playing happily, regardless of the scene.

Nature wields a mighty power.
Coursing through all time with purpose and substance
For those who wish to see its manifestations.
So, like new world necromancers,
The spirits wield this 'great essence' across the vastness of
                                                the earth.
Tap its power and channel to great fusillades of colour,
Magnificence of height and subtlety of texture.
An infinite overlap of wild and cultivated
Tapestries, scattered over every inch.

But, what of these spirits muses the mind.
Elf and fairy are not the things of adulthood.
Whatever dances round my plot,
Drawing out richness and delight,
Can only be a tangible, substantial being for my belief.

I smile and sigh, my pondering revolving, seemingly nowhere.
And standing, muddied in my own fantasy.
Look down and see, smiling back
From the surface of the cold pond,
The spirit of my garden.

W A Prescott

COLOUR IN THE WINTER GARDEN

Gardening books and magazines
Give guidance for the gardener,
On 'colour in the winter garden',
With lists of winter flowering shrubs,
Early bulbs and evergreens.

My winter garden,
Has colours of its own.
And none of these need planting:

White sugar rime
Of hoar frost on old apple trees.

The flare of flame,
Crackling as rose prunings burn,
Blue smoke spiring,
As the fire dies at day's end,
In the cold, still air.

A territorial robin's bobbing breast
And gaudy goldfinch,
Feeding on the last
Seed-heads of lavender.

The fleeting flash
Of a foxes russet coat
And brindled brush,

Breaking cover from the hawthorn hedge
And leaping the long, low wall
In the lowering winter sun.

But the last is rarest and the best,
Bathing all blue-white and magical -
Full moon at midnight.

Christopher Lewis

THE GARDENER

He knows!
That never stultifying look
Holds the sun at gun point.
He reads the weather like a book
And guards his treasure.
Trembling he paces with pride,
The ground a measure of his prize.

He knows!
Those hungry hands hold as much substance
As the soil itself.
Blending recipes of powdered rock without assistance,
Wary of manufactured compounds:
Mastering secrets known only to ecology.
Old and simple.
Scientific grounds would crumble.

But he knows!
With heavy harvest he grows humble.

Alison Hodge

THE GARDENER

Proud pine its deep umbrella green
Shadow casting timeless scene below and time foregone.
The decades dated boughs
Shroud memories, disturb the peace, the grief
of he, the gardener, sight stranded, chair bound, resting
hand on head of faithful guiding hound.
The panama, the stick, the passing calls of children
shadows in the sun.

Roses rampant scented fall, petals pink and red
carpet covering lawn long lost:
Wild strawberries a network spread
where once a cultivated bed.
Broom brazenly outbids the sad remembered
tendrils of a gentle scene of carefully cared for plants.

And time stands still as scents and senses
nudge the corridors of memory.
The gentle heathers, timeless in their struggle to survive
The wilful marigolds and the roses - always roses:
And memory fades - and shades of pine decline
And time stands still.

Pauline Brennan

THE ONION GROWER

Each spring I turn the soil,
And plant these tiny rows of teardrops
in their tough skins.

All the summer long
I water them with love, and shave
the earth of creeping weeds.

As autumn falls, I break
their heavy necks with love, and lay
them down to die in peace.

In winter, when I cook
what was your favourite meal, I cut
their tender hearts, and cry.

Dylan Pugh

In Our Garden

In our garden
The bare branched trees
Seem to be pleading with the sky,
For more light
Than the pale and loitering
January sun can now provide.
And the leaves
Drawn to the earth,
By the weight of winter
Shroud the ground.
But if I look closely,
I see,
The first greening thrusts
From buried bulbs,
Fresh fat green buds
Sprouting on the lilacs,
Strong red tips
Catching fire on the bare
And thorny roses;
Even the old greengage
A well lichened tree,
Is heavy
With budding promise.

Already a soundless
Rebirth is beginning.

George Burns

A GARDENER'S WORLD

There are many stately gardens
in lands both far and near
Where vines entwine and roses climb
that bloom and fade each year.

There are lawns so neat and tidy
with statues here and there
with pots of shrubs and flowers
with names too long, or rare.

There are avenues of Poplars
with fountains either end
'mid balustrades and leafy glades
where shady pathways wend.

And I look at my small garden,
so bleak and cold and grey
with branches blowing in the wind
Another rain filled day.

I glance again, and mid the gloom
I see a gleam of white
A single shining snowdrop
so clean, so brave and bright.

G M Craske

THE GARDEN

There is a garden that I know,
Full of dappled light,
Where almond blossoms fly like snow
Speckling the dark pond below,
With petals white.

Haughty and tall against the wall,
In spring the tulips grow.
In summer roses, beloved by all,
Perfume the air till their petals fall,
When east winds blow.

But nobody lies where blossoms bend low,
And nobody walks on the grass,
There is too much to do, to weed, to mow,
To dig and to hoe, time is the foe
In this Eden alas.

Eva Donaghy

NEW GARDEN

The garden was long and wildly challenging,
And was to be the fulfilment of my father's
Creative horticultural dream.
I was the only member of the family, due to my lack of years,
That wasn't involved in taming that tangled growth.
The air was alive with industry
As my parents and brothers, excavated, weeded, sieved and raked
The hardened soil to a dark and crumbly texture.
On balmy darkening evenings
I would creep from my bed and stand at the opened window,
As they tilled by the light of the moon,
The observer, unobserved by the moonrakers.

It was a long idyllic summer,
And the following year bore
The colour, harmony and design
Of that labour on warm earth.

L J Culbert

THE ALLOTMENT

'Leave them outside,' I said pointing to his wellies.
His spade and fork propped by the back door,
Arms full of carrots and potatoes, and other veg's
His smile said it all. He had brought home the tea.

Gardening is his passion, weeding is his thrill.
His allotment means everything to him,
He talks to me of aphids, greenfly and things,
I just nod in agreement, I don't know what it means.

We tour the garden centres, nearly every week,
Buying bulbs, seeds, slugs, pellets and peat.
But on the bonus side, apart from the fresh veg,
I know just where he will be, always in his shed.

Karen Hullah

WATCHING BOMBUS IN JULY

Liatris, bold with purple feathers,
Spires alive with buzzing bees:
Oblivious of my attention,
Where I sit beneath the trees.

From a nodding blue Campanula,
Robbed of gold with gentle fuss,
To a place of sun and half-shade
Where lies the dappled Dianthus.

Laden from the fragrant Hyssop,
Enters Antirrhinum, but -
Dare she steal the Dragon's nectar
Once that velvet mouth is shut?

Audrey A Greenleaf

THE FAILED GARDENER'S LAMENT

I wish that my flowers (on which I spend hours)
Were like those in the posh magazines,
But my gardening skill is practically nil;
I can't even grow runner beans.

Though my garden shed sags with equipment and bags
Which I send for, from various firms,
My unruly lawn, looking oh! so forlorn,
Is littered with casts from the worms.

My roses have spot and their roots have got rot,
And the grubs they do *so* love a nibble.
Ignorance is not bliss, so please tell me this:
Just what do I do with a dibble?

I have sprayed. I have prayed. I have bought a new spade.
Over compost and weeds I've been slaving.
But now I give up; I shall ring someone up,
And have the lot covered with paving.

Mary Cameron

THE PERSIMMON TREE

It grew in Los Altos, the Persimmon tree,
And offered it's bounty generously.
Like small Chinese lanterns, lit by the sun
It lured the jewelled Humming birds to come.

Tiny black squirrels, acrobatic and quick
Scampered and leapt and chose which to pick,
Then with their forepaws they hugged the best
And carried it down to eat and rest.

They vied with all kinds of exotic birds
Brilliant in colour, too amazing for words,
Which ate of the fruit that glistened and hung
Inviting, and sweet from the heat of the sun.

This pageant took place before very tall trees,
Magnolias and Apricots, and dark green leaves.
While lower grew citrus and strange bright flowers
Enhancing the effect of secret jungle bowers.

All day the sun shone, the sky a glorious blue.
Then darkness hastened, shadows of the darkest hue
Brought out the creatures of the night. Black and white
The skunk appeared, and racoons caught in a beam of light.

Amidst this colour and teeming life, the Persimmon tree
Stood, graceful, silent and proffering free
To all who chose to help themselves, abundance
Of food, juice, and delicate sustenance.

Phyllis Paynter

MY GARDEN

A garden is all peace and beauty,
Or so state the people who know,
A place to think deeply and ponder,
Create calmness and warm inner glow.

But mine seems to wander from normal,
It's a place where work's never complete,
Where I'm digging from Jan to December,
Pulling weeds I can never quite beat.

I have every weed known in this country
And some, I think came from abroad,
They grow vigorously in my topsoil,
And ensure I've no time to get bored.

The insects I've got are horrendous
And immune to all kinds of spray,
They decimate all my good flowers,
Then they pounce on the veggies next day.

The lawns that I laid in my garden,
Are covered in daisies and clover
And my grandchildren's games in the summer
Make calm peaceful moments soon over.

I suppose I must enjoy my garden,
'Cos I spend all my spare time in there,
And it's lovely to sit and drink coffee,
In the sun, with a book, without care.

W R Fyfe

TIME WELL SPENT

Seasons come, seasons go.
Summer sunshine, winter snow,
At times when I cannot sow
God ensures my garden grows.

Constant pulses through the earth
Covered with the greenest turf
Spring is the time for rebirth
Fertile soil now shows its worth.

Hardened soil is upset
Now the rain has made it wet.
Dig in deep. Build up a sweat
And your goal will soon be met.

Make small holes for seeds to sit.
Cover well to protect it
From those avid bluetits
Looking for some nibblets.

Keep an eye on growth to date
Enough water to hydrate
Even though you'll have to wait
A while before they germinate.

Look! A bud has come in view
Silent in the morning dew.
It's just the start of what you
Will see when spring and summer's through.

Fragrant flowers bring sweet scent
To your garden people frequent
Paying the nicest of compliments
A bonus reward for time well spent.

Tessa Mondesir

BEHIND THE SPADE

Our house, it had a secret,
When we moved here years ago.
The paths and lawns were overgrown,
Just weeds and grass on show.

Then as the seasons moved along
We noticed shrubs in bloom
And with the help of spade
And fork, a rake and sturdy broom.

We found a garden, such a dream,
With sun, bright light and shade,
With colourful plants and cool green grass,
Our garden we had made!

Now playing in the greenhouse,
Or planting out our seeds,
Our life is full - quite tiring,
Yes, this plot fills all our needs!

Jennifer Jenkins

GARDEN FANTASY

The garden's a lady's dress,
Fashioned from velvety green,
Where shadows hint at swelling curves,
Sunshine each dart and seam.

The garden's a lady's gown,
Spangled with raindrops, that weep
For a sempstress to sew them round
The hem kissing her feet.

The garden's a lady's stole,
Swinging all ways in the breeze,
With catkins a-dance and a-roll,
Fringing the edge, to tease.

The garden's a lady's shawl,
Close knit in deep-dyed hue;
Forget-me-nots and pansies brawl -
Who's victor - mauve or blue?

The garden's a lady's shroud,
Snowy white, edged with lace.
Gypsophila and alyssum
Caress the marble face.

The garden's an angel's robe,
Starred in the silent night;
Scents, sights and sounds caught in the folds
As the freed soul takes flight.

Beryl M Smith

THE MAGIC GARDEN

My garden is a magical place
Where each season has a changing face.
It is filled with secrets and delight
At morning time, at noon and night.
In spring, the shoots grow green and strong.
The hedges and trees resound with song.
In summer, tall flowers hide the seat
Where one can find a quiet retreat.
In autumn, leaves conceal the ground
Where squirrels and wildlife all abound.
In winter, the moonlight on the snow
Sculptures shapes into an eerie show.

But the crowning glory is, for me,
The life embraced by the tall ash tree.
Its curving branches cast shadows strange
As the garden creates its patterns of change.

Mary Marriott

OUR GARDEN

Oh! The joy of spring-time when behold!
Tender spears break through the earth so cold!
Daffodils regaining life
Away with cruel winter's bitter strife!
Garden beauty starts to unfold.

Oh! garden what dreams we have of you
Flower-filled borders of every hue
Stepping stones among the grass
Garden ornaments we love to pass
Summer-time and our hopes renew.

Along comes autumn both sweet and sad
Though summer's over not all is bad!
Sumptuous fruit once more is here
Sweet red cherry, apple. plum and pear
Thank you, garden, you make us glad!

And so at last dread winter is here
Even though it comes, please do not fear!
Happily we start to plan
That is the lot of every man
Fortunate to have a garden near.

Diana

WITHIN THE EDGES OF MORTALITY

This flower pushed outward
Like a tail of a comet,
Yellow in its feverish beauty
Gulping sweat and tears
Never ravishing art and philosophy
Yet master of both and silence;
And the air full of its aura's energy
A smell that havocs the nostrils
And thirsts a parched tongue;
But what of this beauty
If it be beauty that confines death?

Raymond Fenech

GARDENING AFTER WORK

After the turning of pages
   a turning of the spade

After the glaring tubes
   a glowing sun

After the peering at screens
   a grubbing for weeds

After the recycled air
   an unconditioned wind

After the huge glass cage
   a little greenhouse

After the restless journey
   a gazing at one piece of ground

After the cost justification
   a bountiful soil.

Peter Haslehurst

GARDEN SEASONS

Winter.
Frost edging every leaf.
Silver brushed, star sparkling,
Cotton-wool snow adorning stark tree branches,
Hexagon clusters, soft and perfect.
Fairyland.

Spring.
Spears of green, up-springing
Snowdrop and crocus army leading
Their coloured cohorts all along the border;
Birds, buds and blossoms all proclaiming
Victory.

Summer.
Soft scents and golden sunlight
Flowers slowly opening in continual worship
Of their life-giver, their eternal source;
Presenting symmetry of shape, kaleidoscope of colour.
Joyful days.

Autumn
A rich tapestry, a woven symphony
Of change, of seed-dispersing,
Berry-glowing, seed head scattering
Of the year's toil the end and the beginning,
Fulfilment.

Mary Johnson-Riley

OUR GARDEN

And now the dawn awakes with faithless whispers,
as haunted mists escape into the light,
leaving skein-traps draped upon the willow,
while I choose my thoughts from shades of grey.
Oh, my beloved darling, you lie sleeping
and hear no more the thrush in melody,
mellifluous as ever in our garden,
the murmur-hum of bees and weaving flies,
morning's muted harmony to peace.
Beside our languid pool my life seems tranquil
but autumn thoughts invade my afternoon;
an icy air disturbs the fragile blossoms
and heartless sun invites but moving shadows.
When fearful dusk falls into marish night
I always hear the echo of your laughter
and I must pace your footprints still in love.

Edward Lea

SPRING

The forsythia is yellow,
The sun is coming out,
Buds are on the pussy willow,
Seedlings begin to sprout,
Bulbs are in full flower,
Blossom is about to show,
There's the odd April shower,
That helps the garden grow.

F M Ayling

MY GARDEN

I wake up every morning
To look upon my garden.
And I see beauty and colour and life.

I gaze upon the butterflies
That flit from flower to flower.
And I see beauty and colour and life.

I watch the tiny creatures
That live within the pond.
And I see beauty and colour and life.

I follow the russet leaves
As they drift gently from the trees.
And I see beauty and colour and life.

I stand inside my garden
To watch the season's pass.
And I see beauty and colour and life.

Malcolm Richards

SEASONS

Dew upon the grassy banks, webs of finest silk,
Soft green leaves unfurling, flowers white as milk.
Gentle breezes blowing o'er fields of yellow maize,
The countryside is waiting to greet the springtime days.

Hot sun unrelenting now, sultry, thundery air,
Daisies drooping tiny heads, sadly do they fare.
Rain is falling suddenly, daisy raise your head,
Summertime is here, once more, time has quickly sped.

Leaves are falling to the ground, shades of red and brown,
Farmers looking to the sky, shake their heads and frown,
Summer days are over now, foggy swirls abound,
Autumn brings such awesome, still, strangely muffled sound.

Icy fingers forming on stark and barren trees,
Jack Frost sharply biting at everything he sees,
Cold, crisp days on snow clad hills, hedgerows, too, are white,
Winter clasps the silent earth, day will turn to night.

Flowers, they flourish, tender plants will grow,
As long as all the seasons, surely, come and go.

M O Brazier

A GARDENER'S LAMENT

We try to keep the garden neat but sometimes find it hard.
It's really quite a mammoth feat just to brush the yard.
Both of us work full-time and frequently are tired,
But I feel its such a crime if I'm not inspired
To plant and prune, to dig and delve
By rising moon or sunrise glow.
Especially as the chap next door finds gardening a delight.
He weeds and waters, hoes and sows morning, moon and night
His borders blaze, his lawns are green and smooth as velvet mats,
The sprinkler plays, no weeds are seen, and certainly no cats!
In winter's cold and summer's heat we toil upon our knees,
Bleeding hands and aching feet - but our produce we can freeze.
Onions, carrots, parsnip, swede - they fill our blessed plot
Blooms he has, it is agreed but veggies he has not!
Flowers are fine and please the eye, but better to grow greens,
Blossoms fade and shrubs will die - long live our peas and beans!
So when we see him all the while, inspecting his show winner,
We have to give a little smile - for we can grow our dinner!

Christine A Goodhugh

MY MANTRA - THE GARDEN

Following the veins with the tips of fingers
Feeling its tributaries and edge of leaf
The varied textures, grains and fibres
Or absorbing the pale green
Of soft unfurled new leaves
The smell of herbs and flowers
Or pad of rain on the yielding foliage
Leaving rivulets to slip and darken the bark of trees.

My feet firm on this tiny substance
This plot of my endeavour,
Drinking in the peace that comes
At the end of each exhausting day.

Deirdre van Outersterp

MY GARDEN PLAN

The Christmas tree has been dismantled and planted in the rain,
The decorations packed up until Christmas comes again,
Now it's time to sow the seeds for an early start
So I scan the garden catalogues and plan a work of art.

This year I'll have a cottage garden, like in the olden times
I'd like some scented roses and of course a climbing vine.
How about some honeysuckle and clematis on the wall
Some larkspur, digitalis and hollyhocks that grow up tall.

Sunflowers for the bird seed and sweet peas of every hue
Chrysanthemums and pansies that seem to smile at you,
I'll have mignonette and marigolds, they flower quite a long time,
Then alyssum and asters and pretty aquilegia columbine.

For the vegetables, some lettuce, runner beans and carrots
Tomatoes, potatoes and striped marrows that run riot,
Onions I can always grow but cabbages and sprouts
Always have a nasty fate, for club root is about.

Now I've chosen all my seeds I wait for spring to come
I expect the caterpillars, slugs and snails will undo my plan,
With all the rain my water butts are simply overflowing
All I want now is to see the seeds and flowers growing.

Mollie E Carter

YOUR GARDEN

As you look around the garden on a cold winters day,
You wonder if the bitter wind will ever go away,
It numbs the fingers as you clear the trees of snow,
But you know the snowdrops and crocus will soon begin to show,
Then the daffodils will follow, each the colour of the sun,
And the forget-me-nots, will grow anywhere, just for fun,
Brightly coloured tulips with wallflowers, will stand,
A kaleidoscope of colour, arranged by your own hand,
You know spring has arrived by the cawing of the crows,
As they survey the vegetables, laid out neatly in rows,
The robin, your winter companion, will be up to its old tricks,
Darting right under your spade, for grubs to feed its chicks,
The tiny wren will make a home, in your old potting shed,
While house martins and swallows, swoop and twitter overhead,
Soon summer will begin to show, its more bountiful side,
While toads and frogs will be looking for the shade in which to hide,
Roses in their perfection will preen for all to see,
Mingling their shades and perfume, with the delicate sweet pea,
Delphiniums, the queen of the borders, stand tall,
Surveying their subjects beside the garden wall,
But the clematis looks down from a loftier plain,
Peering over the garden fence, at the ripening grain,
The evening scent of the honeysuckle, still hangs in the air,
Where spiders await to welcome, moths into their lair,

The fruits and berries, hang heavily on the bough,
And autumn descends upon the land, with its usual vow,
That the days will be short and the nights will be chill,
And every creature that lives, must now take its fill,
Soon the frost will glisten, as the moon starts to wane,
And you can settle down, to read your gardening books again.

John R Monk

MY PRIDE AND JOY

It's just a small plot of land
   Of good old Sussex soil,
Tis only on loan to me to tend and care
   The while that I am there.

And if you take the time
   To stand and stare, and lend your ear,
It's full of magic, mystery and life
   The whole of the year.

My helping hand is God's presence there,
   For he sends the frost, the rain and sun,
To help the growth of tiny seeds, to bear
   The miracle and beauty of the flowers to come.

In there season they come,
   The leaves, the fruits and the flowers,
Helped on by the work of the busy bees,
   And visited by butterflies so beautiful to see.

My feathered friends are always round about,
   At my feet the robin hops searching for a morsel to eat,
The blackbird sings in thankfulness it seems,
   For his home around in the trees.

Like unto life its not always a bed of roses,
   There's success and failures and backache and pests,
But then what reward when all springs to new life,
   And later to sit in the garden filled with delight.

Hilda Greenhalf

TUNNEL VISION

Just one mole
Makes a hole
Heap of trouble!

Ann Popple

PRUNING

I find it relaxing
to trim trees and shrubs
or snip the dead heads off the roses.

This cutting back strengthens
and improves the stock
or so every gardener supposes.

Removing the dead wood
encourages growth.
Hard pruning makes crops more abundant

I wonder if my old boss
had this in mind
when lopping me off as redundant.

Cyril Mountjoy

LIKE A POPPY IN THE FIELD

I simply have to stop and look and watch
you move
in the wind the
fragile flowers float

- untouched by storm and rain -
like
islands of amazing red islands
small like scattered rocks on the shore
and large
drifts of fiery red bathing in skylark song

I simply have to stop and stoop and look
at the blush, blushing even
even more deeply
when mingled with
cornflower blue and sweet-smelling white and yellow
bearing the fragrance of summer

I simply have to stop and look and smile
you are like a poppy in the field

Stina de Graaf

WHAT A CHALLENGE

Just another scruffy station
In a sleepy country town.
Thick grass grew on the platform
Causing passengers to frown.
But some said 'It's not long ago
Flowers grew here - made a lovely show.'

Now gone, replaced by nettles,
Matted ivy, brambles tall,
The wretched sight inspired someone
To sound the clarion call:-
'Let's clear this place, some flowers grow.
'T'would be a challenge, that we know.'

For months in weather often bad
We worked, day in, day out.
We dug and trimmed and planted
We pushed on through storm or drought.
Some strange and fearsome tools we used.
Of 'Digging up the platform' we were accused!

At last rewards began to come
As snowdrops, green and white
Were followed by spring flowers
Then the summer show so bright.
The butterflies of brilliant hue
Completed autumn's colours new.

We know this may not last for long,
The weeds may yet return,
Then passengers while waiting
Might for brilliant flowers yearn.
But we've proved this once scruffy place
Can show a very different face.

Gwen Daniels

THOUGH I TRY

The musty smell of rain, on the freshly turned soil,
The twinge of pain one feels, gained from hard work and toil,
The reward that's achieved, with strains and stress applied.
That satisfied feeling; that at least I have tried.

Such experiences, make my garden worth while,
Although much be lacking, in its neatness or style,
Nothing can substitute, any pleasures received,
From fruits of one's labour; satisfaction perceived.

It's not that the harvest, gives me reason to boast
To all types of plant pest, it attracts, like *mine host,*
But just now and again, some miscalculation,
Provides me some success; a great celebration.

The news is then broadcast, to all those who'll give ear.
The story's repeated, at the start of each year,
All those who advise me, I reject with contempt.
As I once again start, to make that final attempt.

Derek Beavis

NEARER GOD'S HEART

Here is my heart's ease -
the garden I have made,
where ancient oak trees
dapple with light and shade
the daisy-studded lawn.
With nectar seeking bees
busy about the hawthorn
flowers, and wood anemones
peep shyly from their bed
of ferns. Where dancing poppies
float upon the wind their red
and crumpled skirts and pansies
smile. And there the tall
enchanted foxglove grows
freckled by a fairy brush,
and loveliest of all
drifts from the hedge
a wild pink rose.

While from the ash tree bough
a thrush
pours out a timeless song.

Yvonne Bulteel

TREES

Two trees were planted close,
and yet for all each might have known, alone,
for both were different sorts,
different leaf and bark and hue;
then one day unsuspecting twig touched
unsuspecting twig, leaf brushed leaf and trees communed.
And slowly as they grew
their boughs and leaves entwined, so loosely
that the slightest wind or breeze could part
and in the rush of wind and youth
one bent towards the other, now away,
and sometimes whispered, sometimes shouted;
yet all the while they grew.
Closer and closer, their branches
entwining, encircling, so each high wind,
would rattle bough on bough,
tear leaf on leaf
ripping and rending each apart
now throwing each together
yet all the while, they grew.
Until one day they found they were as one,
each tree was complimented by each tree,
each bough by bough, each leaf by leaf,
so now when wind blew hard
they did not separate or clash,
but bent together, the one
upheld the other where it weakest was.

Two trees were planted close and closer grew
until each one the other held where're it blow.

Andrew Banfield

THE RELUCTANT GARDENER

What a beautiful garden my visitors say
But they don't have to weed it for hours every day.
It seems horticulture's a permanent fight
Against greenfly and blackfly, ground elder and blight.
From spring through to autumn I battle my way
Destroying invaders with gallons of spray.
I wish I enjoyed it and thought it was fun,
Instead of just something that has to be done.
Last year I was proud of the veg I had sown
But the Somerset wildlife took half what was grown.
The slugs ate the lettuce, the rabbits chose beans,
And a pigeon assault team demolished the greens!
The cows chewed my roses so they're a dead loss
And the patio area's covered with moss.
The shrubs all need pruning and so do the hedges,
When I've finished the lawns I must clip all the edges.
It rained every day for three months in the spring,
Which meant that you couldn't get on with a thing.
But the day that I planted the bedding flowers out
Was to signal the start of a long summer drought.
Whatever the season the weather's not right
I'm sure Mother Nature just does it for spite.
I welcome the winter, I greet it with glee,
It means I don't have to go gardening you see
What really delights me are blankets of snow
For it all looks so tidy and nothing can grow.
I dream of retirement, a cottage quite small,
And to make it just perfect - no garden at all!

Jenny Holmes

TAKEN FOR GRANTED

Just look at the garden of our neighbours
The state of the beds really reflects their behaviour!

Never a rake or spade in hand they have taken
Since moving to this street here in Strathaven.

Plenty people would for a garden wish hard
To tend for and care; their very own *farmyard*.

But here we see some who take for granted
A pleasure of nature, but as yet unplanted.

G Milne

MY GARDEN OF MEMORIES

I've a garden of memories
A mish mash of pleasure,
Plants in abundance
To cherish and treasure.

A fuschia from Alice
I don't know its name,
It made so many cuttings
Now I've lots all the same.

Two shrubs came from Betty
And that plant in the pond,
The bird box Dad made
And the one just beyond.

See that bit of yellow
By the well it's quite new,
It's next door Freda's
with the violets too.

The snowdrops from Julie
The marsh marigold from Ann,
The heebee from Sylvia
They are all in the plan.

From Sally came rock roses
Mike gave me the seat,
Lots visit my mish mash
Over full and not neat.

No sprays nothing harmful
All cheerfully blends,
My garden my haven
All given by friends.

Beryl Osborne

A GARDENER'S ACROSTIC

G iving joy and happiness to all those who are there,
   letting Mother Nature's beauty shine in a world where it is
   often neglected or ignored.

A ll year 'round new things to enjoy,
   plants, flowers, trees of all shapes and sizes.
   Each brings a smile to tired faces.

R aindrops clean and refresh this place,
   glittering diamonds on the incomparable beauty of a rose
   petal. Little tears shed for a world so determined to
   destroy.

D ewy mornings when the air is clean and all is new.
   Such times are for solitude but never loneliness,
   for this place is alive with activity and song.

E den, a personal paradise is created,
    with colours and aromas that tease your senses
    and evoke memories of other times and places.

N o place, no where could ever come close
    to this haven from the frightening reality of
    a world slowly dying. The place?
    My garden of course.

Aoife Toomey

THEN GOD A GARDEN MADE

When Dan took on the garden
'Twas in a sorry state -
All overgrown with weeds and bine
From house to broken gate.

He slaved all day from dawn to dusk
Unless it poured with rain,
And even then he worked on plans
To get it straight again.

At last it was in order,
And when the summer came
Dan's garden drew admiring looks
And he, some local fame.

The vicar, passing by one day,
Congratulated Dan,
And said what wonders God could do
When He assisted man.

'Maybe,' growled Dan, with blistered hands
And aches in every bone,
'But perhaps you should have seen it
When He did it on His own!'

Marion Brisley

EARTH

Please lay me in the earth
where my fingers have plunged,
felt its grainy moisture
harshly pulled, gently planted.
This earth that I have loved.

My spade has cut it
guillotining hardness
its weight bending my back.
Mountain ranges left by my labours
exposing worms, anaemic and fat
disorientated, defenceless in the light.
The robin waits watching.

Cavernous holes left by
unwillingly transplanted bushes
filled by newcomers
their roots spreading in the compost
carried on the spade,
the trail seen across the lawn.
Daffodil bulbs lying exposed, aliced
their whereabouts forgotten
quickly covered by tumbling weeds,
green dampness drying in the wind.
Ladybirds scramble for safety.

As I dig
neighbours stop in the passing
dogs smile, inviting caress.
Above, the rufus feathered kestrel
its descend as straight as a rod.
Safe in the willow tree
sparrows and tits perch momentarily
seeing, but unseen, by the cat.

This dark heaviness holds no fear
for life begins within it
kingdoms supporting other empires.
Please lay me in it when I die.

Susanne Shalders

BEHIND THE SPADE

Behind the spade the gardener stands,
Deep in thought, with experienced eye;
Brushing soil from workworn hands,
Regards the scene from earth to sky.

In his mind the plan appears,
An arbour here, a pool just there -
And quickly more and more ideas
crowd to the growing vista fair.

A graceful birch atop a mound,
Snowdrops, heathers, to dance in spring;
A twisting path to curve around
The fine green lawn - and birds to sing.

Baskets on an old stone wall
Flowing with reds and golds and blues,
Wooden seats where one and all
Can sit and linger, drink the views.

Russet leaves on shrubs and trees
When summer fades and autumn comes,
Hazy days and lazy bees
Round up the last of pollen thrums

Striking shapes of fir trees gold
And green and blue, when winters snow
Falls soft, to keep the ground from cold
When only Christmas roses show.

All this and more the gardener sees;
If he only had the ground to turn
His thoughts into realities,
Instead he can only dig and yearn,

While caring for his little plot -
- A small allotment's all he's got.

Cynthia Bach

THE PERFECT GARDEN

The perfect garden, flowers in bloom
Lawn and hedges neatly hewn
A pond with gurgling fountain stream
Weeds all gone, none can be seen

No leaves upon the garden shed
And on the bushes no *dead heads*
The gravel path within its bounds
Here no moles dare to make a mound

Hanging baskets, borders too
All have colours matched in hue
Asters blend, roses contrast
A garden full of skill and art

But this garden with contempt I view
As its every need is tended to
You may think this is strange behaviour
But it's the garden of my neighbour!

Helen Dodd

CHILDHOOD MEMORIES

His bedding plants in full flower
Their colours bright and clear
I remember everything lovely in that year
I chased after all the butterflies
And caught them in a net
A memory in my later life
I think of with regret
Lobelia, chrysanthemum all the marigolds
Bring back childhood memories
As my mind unfolds
He chased me with a snapdragon
Making the flower open and close
I ran off down the garden path
To where he grew a rose
New dawn with its aroma
A delicate beautiful pink
I tried to make some perfume
But heavens what a stink
Dahlias, honeysuckle, standard fuchsias too
He called them dancing ladies
If you look they do
This man he was my grandfather
I miss him oh so much
And what he could have taught me
With his green-fingered touch

But I do the best I can
I work hard and I strive
To recreate those memories
And keep his dreams alive.

Terry Kearney

MY HAVEN OF PEACE

The bees sip on the honeysuckle,
beside the garden gate.
The lobelia and white alyssum
edge the pathway grey and straight.

The scented summer roses,
in shades of pink and white,
are undersown with pansies,
their rainbow colours bright.

Tall spiky salvias jostle
with geraniums flaming red.
Together with french marigolds
they share a fiery bed.

Hanging baskets overflow
with begonias large and small.
Pale ballet dancing fuchsias
cascade against the wall.

If ever I feel troubled
or my world's turned upside down.
I sit out in my garden.
It's the best cure, I have found.

Sylvia Dodds

A PROMISE OF SPRING

A night's cruel frost and now the leaves lie thickly,
a multicoloured tapestry, awaiting the rake.
It is late November;
but before the unfurling of a single Witchhazel bloom
- as curious as a deformed spider -
are revealed the grey tips of snowdrops,
white at heart and full of promise,
peering out from behind the curtain of the year's end.
Barely winter, yet already spring's foot is in the door.
Gladdening the heart, lifting the spirits,
until I scent again the rose of summer,
amidst spiralling honeysuckle and stately lily.

Michelle Loetz

THE GARDEN'S OUR PLEASURE

The garden's our pleasure,
A place to sit in our moments of leisure.
Somewhere we go to enjoy the sun,
To relax when our days work is done.
There's bees buzzing 'round the flowers so sweet,
Doesn't it all look a wonderful treat.
Lobelia, alyssum bizzie lizzie and daisy,
It all makes you feel everso lazy.
But you can't sit too long
'Cause the weeds start growing,
And of course the grass will need mowing.
There's always something to keep you busy,
You get so you're running 'round in a tizzy.
It's wonderful to have the sun,
Now the watering must be done.
Our friends the slimy slugs
And all those awful little bugs
Munch their way through our greens
Trying to spoil our garden dreams.

But it's all worth while you must agree
Just look at that prize sweet pea.
Colours around us everywhere
Scent of flowers in the air.
Everyday a new sight to treasure,
There's no doubt about it -
The garden's our pleasure.

Muriel Cooper

GOOD PROGRAMMING

A microdot is put to rest in soil:
its blueprint for high branches, twigs and leaves
help it soak in water, build up strength
to burst back like a jack-in-the-box one day.

Then roots give power to push and shove
towards an encouraging sun that smiles down help
on colouring leaves that spread out strong:
they're scalped by the wind that whistles past.

The stem becomes a trunk as years go by,
indicating time to concentrate on fruit:
fleshy packages protecting seeds
that will fall to start this cycle once again.

Peter Comaish

DESTRUCTION

It was a small flower among the weeds
Hopeful, vibrant and alive.
It held a pristine beauty, beyond the seven
wonders of the world,

Bleak and bitter winter, lashing rain and
crashing August thunder,
Have wrecked their tragic bloody ruin.
Tattered gentle petals, lie crushed beyond repair,
Shattered by the jackboots of time and wretched
circumstance.

Susan Mary Heggie

A FLEETING VISIT

The garden is alive and bright,
Bird songs soar through golden light,
As friendly blue-tit swoops and dips,
Winging through the fragrant air.
It lands, watching me from distant perch
Its 'round white face slashed back
With the bandit mask of black.

Quietly I dig my carrot patch,
As now the blue-tit dives to catch,
A worm uncovered by my panting labours,
My garden companion wins its favours,
The soil laid bare, my work is done,
And blue-tit flies off into setting sun.

P J Reed

UNTITLED

In a corner of my garden
Where the sleeping hedgehogs lie
Beneath the fall of autumn leaves
To pass the winter by.

In a corner of my garden
Where pots stand cracked and bare
Beneath the arms of naked tree
In sadness and despair.

In a corner of my garden
Where I hardly ever tread
Beneath the soil there breathes the Spring
To plant life in the dead.

In a corner of my garden
Where weeds are left to grow
Beneath the shade of winter sun
The snowdrops start to show.

Rachael Robinson

A LILY FLOWER

A single lily flower
Unfolds its beauteous face;
This purest virgin bloom
Reflects Madonna's grace.

Parchment petals open
Translucent as a pearl.
Perfection, nature's art,
Her mysteries unfurl.

Wafted in the breezes
A fragrance honey-sweet;
Freshened by the raindrops,
Strengthened by the heat.

Held in trembling fingers
By the silk-soft bride.
Sent in fond remembrance
For one who sadly died.

This single lily flower
Awakes my senses all.
It speaks to me of love
And holds me in its thrall.

Jeanne Webb

THE SOIL

For years I worked with you
Looked after you
Took care of you
Avoided treading on you
In the pouring rain
Put manure onto you
Put manure into you
Hoed off your invading weeds.

I made you a good home for plants
I planted pretty things
I planted edible things
I taught people how to look after you
I sowed seed
I sowed and mowed your grass.

I made your structure long lived,
Whole, solid,
I added manure.

Now
On a grey day in October
As the season closes down
I ride into town on the local bus
I look up at the cemetery on the hill
I think of the soil
And bulky organic matter.

Liam Keating

ODE TO A TOMATO

Just like a mighty oak tree
that's from the acorn grown
the succulent red tomato
from the tiny pip is sown.

I pop you in my growbag
inside my greenhouse warm
to protect you from the elements
the sun the wind and storm.

Tomatoes are very hard to grow
you tend them but you never know
if they will suffer from hollow fruit
                        or blossom drop
or even worse from buckeye rot.

I water them regularly, but as a treat
I give them potash once a week
I love to watch the fruitlets swell
until they're red and looking well.

The best time is the salad season
when at last I have a reason . . .
to pick them!

Kate Roberts & Linda Terry

THE HIDDEN GARDEN

When I was a child, I would often roam,
through fields and down lanes, away from my home.
One day when lost, I came to a wall and
started to climb this Eiffel so tall.
There in front of me, plain as could be,
was the loveliest garden I ever did see.
A fountain played music to the sound of the bees,
the wind blew softly throughout the trees.
A sundial stood silently, counting the hour,
a dandelion clock, competed for power.
Pink, purple and white stood the hollyhocks,
as golden alyssum danced on the rocks,
A butterfly beat on a dahlia drum,
the birds sung sweet and the bees did hum.
Campanula bells played along with the band,
peonys waltzed by, hand in hand.
Asters like pom poms, shook their heads,
in front of resplendent, herbaceous beds.
The fragrance of myrtle wafted around,
to this lovely garden's sights and sounds.
Roses in red, pink, yellow and white,
climbed and rambled out of my sight.
But the most impressive and best of all,
was Joseph's coat draped over a wall.
As the sun goes down and shadows arrive,
I sit in my garden, where memories thrive,
of that wondrous sight on that summers day,

when I went down the lane and lost my way.
Now I open my eyes, dusk to await
and see that beautiful garden, I did recreate.

Susi Howell

OF MOLES AND MEN

Moles and men are not great friends, I know.
My neighbour is especially unfond of them;
They have made some ugly hills in his garden.

'The best way to kill a mole,' he blusters,
'Is to catch him working near the surface,'
(He lowers his voice so the moles won't hear us)
'Now, the freshest hill is the one you're interested in,' (I'm not)
'Dusk is the best time . . . shotgun loaded and cocked.
You have to look sharp. And when you see one particle
Of soil twitch - pull the trigger . . . and that's it.
The shock, you see.' (He eyes me narrowly)
'Much more humane, in my opinion, than traps or poison,
Why, look at their fine fur coats - hardly a mark on them.'

Oh yes, I can see them plainly - all seven of them;
Small aliens from the underground element.
Hanged by their poor snouts from the barbs of his fence,
Dead as dead; empty as moleskin purses.
Tiny pink palms, splayed out,
Made for swimming through rich, dank earth.

Now I do not extol the virtues
Of moles to men, or men to moles;
But it seemed a sorry end to see them dangling there,
In the thin, insipid spring air.
But moles and men are not great friends, I know.

C Gent Drummond